AMERICA IN DENIAL

SUNY series in African American Studies

John R. Howard and Robert C. Smith, editors

AMERICA

in

DENIAL

How Race-Fair Policies
Reinforce Racial Inequality in America

LORI LATRICE MARTIN

SUNY
PRESS

Cover image by Dan Brandenburg / iStock.com

Published by State University of New York Press, Albany

© 2021 State University of New York

For information, contact State University of New York Press, Albany, NY
www.sunypress.edu

Library of Congress Cataloging-in-Publication Data

Name: Martin, Lori Latrice, author.
Title: America in denial : how race-fair policies reinforce racial inequality in
   America / Lori Latrice Martin, author.
Description: Albany : State University of New York Press, [2021] | Series:
   SUNY series in African American Studies | Includes bibliographical references
   and index.
Identifiers: ISBN 9781438482972 (hardcover : alk. paper) | ISBN 9781438482965
   (pbk. : alk. paper) | ISBN 9781438482989 (ebook)
Further information is available at the Library of Congress.

10 9 8 7 6 5 4 3 2 1

In Memory of
Johnnie G. McCann and Kenneth O. Miles

Contents

Acknowledgments

I am forever grateful for the support of the following individuals throughout the development of *America in Denial: How Race-Neutral Policies Reinforce Racial Inequality in America*: Lee and Edith Burns, Emily and John Thornton, Rachel Nichols, Stephen C. Finley, Biko Mandela Gray, Roland Mitchell, Linda Smith Griffin, Juan Barthelemy, Maretta McDonald, Landon Douglas, Sarah Becker, Annemarie Galeucia, Ifeyinwa Davis, John Aggrey, Walter Holliday, Nikki Fargas, C. Keith Harrison, Advancement of Blacks in Sports (ABIS), Black Student Athletes Association (BSAA) at LSU, Black Scholars Roundtable in Sports, Derrick Martin Jr., David I. Shannon Rudder, Hayward Derrick Horton, John Sibley Butler, Dorothea Swann, Bobbie Commodore, Frances Pratt, Dominique Dillard, Mahalia Howard, Ashley Maryland, David and Shannon Rudder, Ewart Forde, Constance Slaughter Harvey, Michael Rinella, and Emir Sykes.

Introduction

The refusal to acknowledge that a problem exists and persists does not mean the problem is not real and it certainly doesn't mean that it will somehow cease being a problem without one or more interventions. Refusing to adequately address enduring racial disparities on many issues results in a host of actual and metaphorical deaths, which may best be understood as death by denial. Far too many Americans have arrived at the conclusion that efforts to adequately compensate black people for the discrimination they faced (and continue to face) is unfair to present-day white people and/or "politically unfeasible" and is, therefore, not worth the fight. White privilege, some argue, is not experienced equally by whites, as evidenced in variations in outcomes by gender, for example. Moreover, poor white people, regardless of gender, and more affluent whites have little in common, others have claimed.

The idea of white disadvantage extends further; it extends to the idea that white people are actually one of the most at-risk groups in America. White people are believed to be at risk due to perceived black progress and external threats ranging from terrorism to illegal immigration, among other claims. This was on full display in Charlottesville in 2017 and the Unite the Right rally. Protestors gathered to contest the removal of a monument to Confederate General Robert E. Lee. The protests resulted in the death of Heather Heyer, who was killed when a supporter of the rally deliberately drove into a crowd of counterprotesters (Sweeny 2019). The belief that whites are at risk has seemingly increased over the past decade and has politically energized many white Americans, including around such themes as Make America Great Again.

The consequences of these developments are many and are not limited to upticks in overt manifestations of white supremacy, such as in the case of the burning of historic black churches, but also include a potentially

1

dangerous and harmful decline in commitments to speak truth to power
when the issue is 1) clearly about race and 2) involves the experiences of
black people in America.

Various groups ranging from white liberals to selected black scholars
and black politicians are among the former freedom fighters that have
seemingly thrown their hands up in surrender and tossed in the proverbial towel. Former advocates for the rights of historically disadvantaged
groups appear to have traded in their social activist credentials for the
opportunity to become proponents of programs and proposals that defy
history, logic, and hundreds of years of scholarly research and embrace
the existence or emergence of a race-fair America.

The types of programs and policies advocated by these perform-
ers—influential individuals promoting changes they claim are beneficial
to black people but will actually set black people back—have been shown
not only to do more harm than good to black people but also simultaneously provide additional benefits to already advantaged groups. Some
black scholars have become closely associated with this latest iteration of
colorblindness as demonstrated in their push for a program that would issue
bonds to every newborn in America as a way to address persistent racial
wealth inequality. The scholars are among a high-profile group claiming
race-neutral policies and programs provide the greatest chances for the
creation of a race-fair America. These claims persist despite decades of
research that point to the role that antiblack sentiments had in creating,
transforming, and perpetuating a racialized social structure that remains
fully intact even today and will remain intact for the foreseeable future.

Black people continue to bear the brunt of the blame for enduring
racial disparities in virtually every area of social life from wealth, education,
health, to crime. Efforts claiming to address such issues, particularly those
adhering to the idea of a race-fair America, tend to focus on pathology
of blackness that is rooted in antiblack sentiment. Consequently, related
solutions to racial disparities call for behavior modifications that will lead
to conformity with mythical so-called white middle-class standards. At the
same time, current so called race-fair solutions to racial disparities also
direct attention away from the need for systemic changes and the need
for the erasure of antiblack sentiments from both the American psyche
and social fabric.

The road to a race-fair America is paved with universal programs,
which are: 1) focused primarily on behavioral modifications, 2) open to

all, and 3) claim to benefit the common good. There are a number of problems with this line of thinking.

First, the root of America's race problem is the systematic exclusion of black people in all areas of social life. Second, the term *common* was never meant to (and still does not) include black people. Third, the material and nonmaterial harms done to black people that are still felt today must be acknowledged. Just compensation is long overdue. Fourth, the idea that programs that are available to all people will necessarily benefit black people has been shown time and time again not to be the case.

Millions of black people have been in (and are still caught in) a disadvantage feedback loop, whereby generations of black people suffer the effects of antiblack practices and policies. These practices and policies tend to enrich members of the dominant racial group both literally and figuratively. This exploitation and exclusion is not new, but it is a fact some wish to forget, or chose to ignore, for reasons unknown. Doing what is right is not something that any individual or group should give up so easily. The right thing to do is to be truthful about the origins of racial disparities in America on a host of sociological outcomes. The causes of racial disparities in wealth, education, and the criminal justice system in America are varied but tend to include one of two dominant narratives: culture versus structure.

Culture versus Structure

CULTURAL EXPLANATIONS

Culture arguments tend to focus on the need for behavior modifications for individuals and groups. A number of classic as well as contemporary research studies exemplify this approach to explaining historic and contemporary racial disparities on a host of sociological outcomes. Oscar Lewis's "The Culture of Poverty" is one of the most cited studies and, by his own account, one of the most misunderstood. Lewis attempted to explain why poverty persists and distinguishes simply being poor from living within a culture of poverty (Lewis 1966). In fact, Lewis made the argument that it would be easier to end poverty than to eliminate the culture of poverty. Lewis like many others focused on culture, centered whiteness, viewed blackness as pathological, and both acknowledged and minimized the role of structure and structural processes. For example, although Lewis was engaged in research on Puerto Rican households in Puerto Rico and New York, he returned a number of times to discussions about black households as if the so-called culture of poverty was normative for black people; even if it was not normative for black people, Lewis understood that belief as part of the conventional wisdom held by the general (white) population and among (white) scholars. Lewis (1966) was concerned that some, particularly in the mass media, have misused the concept in such a way as to see a culture of poverty as a necessarily bad thing as opposed to perhaps a coping strategy for dealing with economic reality. Lewis (1966) did acknowledge the interaction of racial discrimination and economic disadvantage in his work and how those factors inform the black experience in distinctive ways, but he signaled that the best way to address poverty is through modifications in behavior as evidenced in his discussion about the role of social work and social workers.

Daniel Patrick Moynihan's (1965) report about the black family in the mid-1960s is another example of works that placed cultural explanations at the center of arguments about differences between black and white people in America. Indeed, Moynihan (1965) famously, or infamously, declared the state of the black family a national crisis. Moynihan (1965) tried to evaluate black families using what could be framed as ideal types of white families as the standard. Moynihan (1965) also (mis)used the work of black scholars, like black sociologist E. Franklin Frazier, to support his claims that a deficient culture caused the disruption and disorganization of the black family in such a way that governmental intervention was required. Moynihan (1965), and others have cited Frazier's (1939) work on the black family and used it as a justification for claims of the existence of the pathology of blackness. It is clear that neither Moynihan (1965), nor many others misreading Frazier (1939), have read, or are even aware, of Frazier's 1927 work. In the late 1920s publication, Frazier (1927) described the pathology of prejudice. His focus was on the pathology of white people's prejudices and discriminatory actions toward black people. Frazier (1927) described how seemingly rational, law-abiding white people responded in the face of perceived black progress, for example. This publication should have been an early call for scholars to focus not on the perceived pathology of black families, and of blackness more broadly, but on whiteness, as Pattillo (2005) later suggests in her review of sociological literature on black middle-class neighborhoods.

Herbert Gans (1979) was another scholar whose work addressed the role of culture in understanding different outcomes by race. Gans's (1979) focus was centered on a concept he called symbolic ethnicity. Gans (1979) argued that some scholars were misinterpreting and misusing concepts such as ethnicity and culture when they were actually addressing what he called class behavior. Gans (1979), in his exploration of how assimilation and acculturation functioned across generations, argued against the commonly shared wisdom of the day regarding ethnicity. Many scholars proclaimed that American society was in the midst of a revival of renewed interest in ethnicity. Gans (1979) made the argument that the acculturation and assimilation that white immigrants from places like Southern, Central, and Eastern Europeans arriving between the 1880s and early 1920s experienced were ongoing and that later generations of white ethnic groups were merely using ethnic symbols. Later generations had little use for ethnic cultures or ethnic organizations, which some scholars argued were central to the assimilation of earlier white immigrants into whiteness and thus into mainstream society. Gans (1979) further argued that the absence, or weakness, of similar institutions in nonwhite communities, including black communities, was responsible, at least in part, to their inability to assimilate.

Gans described the symbolic ethnicity among later generations as "an ethnicity of last resort" (1979, 1). He also argued that what some scholars have regarded as "ethnicity is largely a working-class style" (Gans 1979, 2). He further contended that black progress was viewed as threats to white working-class style, not ethnicity. For Gans, "ethnicity can sometimes serve as a convenient euphemism for anti-black endeavors" (1979, 2). Class interests, not ethnicity, compelled white ethnic groups to fight against black demands.

Ethnicity has become over time, for Gans (1979), more voluntary. Examples of ethnic symbols are rites of passage, holidays, and involvement in national and international political issues involving a country of origin. Gans (1979) described the old country as an identity symbol. Such symbols, and symbolic culture more broadly, function in service to practiced culture. "Ethnic behavior, attitudes, and even identities are, however, determined not only by what goes on among the ethnics but also by developments in the larger society" (Gans 1979, 15).

Structural Explanations

Wilson's (1978, 1987) works about the black middle class and the underclass led to a cottage industry of studies aimed at either supporting or refuting his major theses. Critics of his work tend to advance structural explanations in understanding racial disparities on many sociological variables. Drawing upon structural arguments is not new. Surely, one can find notable scholars, such as W. E. B. Du Bois (1995), arguing that the experiences of black people in America were not due to the inherent inferiority of black people or because their socialization lacked the necessary cultural tools for success. While Du Bois (1995) certainly acknowledged differences in behaviors and attitudes among black people, and between black and white people, he understood them to be direct consequences of broader structural issues. Despite living in one of the nation's most violent times, Du Bois (1995) did not wholly concede to conservative untruths. Du Bois's many studies, including *The Philadelphia Negro* and others, pointed to the roles of public policies and private practices in understanding the experiences of black people.

Likewise, for all of the work connecting Frazier (1937) and Moynihan (1965) to the pathology of black culture arguments, Frazier's body of work includes several studies where he stresses the role of structure over culture. In 1937, Frazier published his study about black people living in Harlem and how the city developed into various zones based in part on the socioeconomic status of the inhabitants. His book *Black Bourgeoisie* showed how the black middle class had a distorted view of itself and its importance to black people, and to the broader American society. Frazier (1957) cited some structural barriers that kept the black middle class from separating themselves from poorer black people and kept them from assimilating into (white) mainstream society. Frazier's (1957) focus on limited access to certain financial markets, his understanding of how even historically black colleges and universities (HBCUs) were funded and how their curriculum was designed, demonstrated his understanding about the significance of the social structure and black people's place in it.

Robert Blauner, in *Racial Oppression in America*, advanced structural explanations for understanding why race still mattered in the country at the time of his writing. Blauner (1972) made the provocative claim that one could understand the relationship between black and white people in the United States much like that of the relationship between an empire and a colonized nation. According to Blauner (1972), as in the conventional definition, the dominant racial group in America used such things as military force, infusions of capital, and so on, to dominate every aspect of black life. The only difference was that the two groups were occupying the same physical space. Blauner (1972) referred to the relationship as internal colonialism. Mario Barrera (1979), author of *Race and Class in the Southwest*, extends Blauner's work in his examinations of Chicanos in the Southwest region of the United States from the period following the Mexican-American War through the first three quarters of the twentieth century.

In a similar sense, Ture and Hamilton (1992), authors of *Black Power*, highlighted how the structures of institutions yield differences in access and differences in rewards by race. Ian Haney López (2000) built upon the idea of institutional racism by focusing on what some scholars call "new institutionalism" (1723). This concept "rejects the rational action theories that animate so much of the social sciences. Instead, new institutionalism posits that frequently repeated but largely unexamined social practices and patterns at once structure and give meaning to human interaction" (Haney López 2000, 1723). In other words, structure matters and *may* include "both cognitive and cultural components" (1723). Haney López (2000) stressed the importance of a continued focus on structural forces to understand the enduring racial divide in America. "To talk of *institutional* racism may be to engage in dry analysis, but to posit institutional *racism* places at center stage our responsibility to address largely unrecognized processes of organizational and social life that harm our society" (Haney López 2000, 1844).

Michael Omi and Howard Winant (1994) offered a new way of theorizing about race and understanding enduring black-white differences in the early 1990s with the publication of their book *Racial Formation in the United States*. Omi and Winant provided a thorough and helpful review of race theories, over time, beginning with the ethnicity paradigm. This paradigm experienced three major phases. The first phase came as a response to biological views about race. The second was dominated by themes of assimilation and cultural pluralism. The third phase was in defense of what Omi and Winant (1994) categorized as conservative egalitarianism against radical assaults on group rights.

Omi and Winant (1994) cautioned against the treatment of race as merely a by-product of ethnicity, or as the same as ethnicity. Instead, Omi and Winant understood race as "a concept, which signifies and symbolizes social conflicts and interests by referring to different types of bodies" (1994, 55). Racial formation, which Omi and Winant described as a two-step process, involved "the sociohistorical process by which racial categories are created, inhabited, transformed, and destroyed (1994, 55). The first step includes "projects in which human bodies and social structures are represented and organized" (Omi and Winant 1994, 55). The second step links racial formation to the evolution of hegemony.

Eduardo Bonilla-Silva had high praise for the work of Omi and Winant, and for other sociologists studying race, but also offered important critiques regarding previous scholarship on race and race relations in America. In "Rethinking Racism," Bonilla-Silva (1997) said theories about racism stressed social and systematic qualities of racism and the structured nature of whiteness but did not account for racially stratified societies. Moreover, Bonilla-Silva (1997) argued that racial formation gave a lot of attention to political, ideological, and cultural processes. Bonilla-Silva (1997) attempted to develop a structural theory of racism that addressed the limitations of existing works about race. He cited seven important limitations. First, racism was not understood as an integral part of the foundation of the social structure. Second, racism was far too often considered as psychological and studied at the individual level. Third, racism, argued Bonilla-Silva, was framed as unchanging, such that rearticulation of racism was viewed as reductions, or as declines. Fourth, racism was defined as irrational. Additionally, racism was thought to only manifest in overt ways. Sixth, some scholars, argued Bonilla-Silva, had mistakenly treated racism as a historical artifact. Seventh, still other scholars had set-forth circular arguments whereby "racism is established by racist behavior, which itself is proved by the existence of racism" (1997, 469).

Bonilla-Silva (1997) presented the idea of the racialized social system, which described societies that were structured, at least in part, by grouping actors by racial groups and the racial groups were socially based. Racial phenomena are the expected outcome of a racialized social system (Bonilla-Silva 1997). Racism can change in nature and may be overt or covert. Racial behavior, contended Bonilla-Silva (1997), was rational and the reproduction of the racialized social system was connected to contemporary structures and not just to the past. Bonilla-Silva (1997) held that his structural theory of racism could account for the emergence, transference, and disappearance of such things as stereotypes.

Clearly, Bonilla-Silva (1997) and other scholars acknowledged the importance of understanding the ways in which society is structured and structured along racial lines as significant in explaining the experiences of black and white people in the United States. Bonilla-Silva's (1997) willingness to unapologetically confront conservative untruths was much appreciated and likely accounts for his continued popularity among critical sociologists. Although, as previously stated, Wilson (1991) called upon scholars to be brave and make structural arguments, he wanted to soften the blow by conceding to a more conservative thesis even when the research did not bear it out. Surely, the process of publishing and being part of the national debate on any subject matter is political, but popularity should not dictate the important work sociologists must do.

Cultural and Structural Arguments Combined

In *The Declining Significance of Race*, William Julius Wilson (1978) focused on how structural and economic changes, particularly after the civil rights movement, impacted the black population. One impact was the extent to which class increased in importance as a determinant of the life chances and life opportunities of black people. According to some of Wilson's (e.g., 1987) later writings, he regretted not devoting more attention to what he called the underclass and offering related policy recommendations. The underclass was a term Wilson (1987) used to describe a relatively large group within the black population at the bottom of the American social structure with relatively low levels of education and low wages. Wilson's (1987) book *The Truly Disadvantaged* was an attempt to address the oversight. Wilson made the argument in *The Truly Disadvantaged* that the problems facing inner cities "cannot be accounted for by the easy explanation of racism" (1987, ix).

Before the 1960s, Wilson argued, inner-city communities, which are disproportionately black, were areas where there was "positive neighbor-hood identification, and explicit norms and sanctions against aberrant behavior" (1987, 3). Due to the loss of jobs and a mass exodus out of the inner city by working- and middle-class black role models, those left behind had to deal with the social situation into which they were born and adapted to it in ways that created self-perpetuating pathology, said Wilson (1987). Wilson's arguments about black people and the role that culture played in understanding racial disparities are reminiscent of Lewis's work on the culture of poverty.

Wilson (1987) also commented about the impact of Moynihan's (1965) scholarship about race and the role of culture in understanding black and white differences on a host of social issues. Wilson made the case that reactions to the Moynihan report scared many scholars away from focusing on culture as the dominant explanation for understanding the overrepresentation of black people among the poor and on other negative sociological outcomes. The effects were, according to Wilson, felt for more than ten years. Conservative explanations about the absence of group values and the impact of government programs on individual and group behavior became dominant in discussions about black people without more nuanced discussions about the complexity of culture. Black families and individuals existed outside the mainstream American occupational system for Wilson. These folks, argued Wilson, "lack training and skills and either experience long-term unemployment or are not members of the labor force, individuals who are engaged in street crime and other forms of aberrant behavior, and families that experience long-term spells of poverty and/or welfare dependency" (1987, 2).

Although Wilson (1987) seemed to understand the role that structural factors played in the experiences of people living in inner-city communities, particularly black people, he nevertheless portrayed economically disadvantaged black people, at best, as deviant and at worst as criminals. Wilson's default argument was one that privileged culture. Wilson called upon more liberal scholars and thinkers to be more proactive and bolder about their claims that cultural values emerge as the result of a particular set of social circumstances and life chances, and life opportunities reflect one's class and racial position. Wilson (1987) was willing to make some concessions to become part of a national conversation and contribute to public discourse about the linkages between cultural values, race, and class. One major concession involved the participation of scholarship and dialogue that reflected both liberal and conservative views more equally. Wilson was, in essence, telling liberal scholars and thinkers that if they wanted to be heard then they have to be willing to concede that there are merits to the conservative thesis and address what he considered "the dynamic interplay between ghetto-specific cultural characteristics and social and economic opportunities" (1987, 18). Wilson assessed the political landscape and conceded that it was not only politically feasible to dismiss conservative views, in many ways he embraced them. Wilson's (1978) work has arguably had more of an impact on the field of sociology and beyond since the publication of *The Declining Significance of Race* than any sociologist in America on the subjects of cultural values, race, and class.

Mark Gould (1999) saw the problem of disciplinary flip-flopping—acknowledging structural explanations about race but privileging cultural explanations—on issues not only among people like William Julius Wilson but also scholars such as John Ogbu. Ogbu is well known for his research about race and education (Gould 1999). Gould showed how both scholars routinely made structural arguments to explain racial phenomena but regularly returned to culture of poverty arguments. Gould (1999) attributed this intellectual dance to a failure on the part of Wilson, Ogbu, and others to distinguish between normative and cognitive expectations. Gould (1999) flat out refuted Wilson (1987) when he stated, "Inner-city blacks are not enmeshed in a 'culture of poverty'" (1999, 172). He further noted, "Wilson apparently wants to both reduce ghetto-specific culture to the social situation that produces it, thus making it malleable to the face of situational change, and to see it as self-perpetuation in the face of structural change" (1999, 174).

Similarly, Ogbu, according to Gould (1999), characterized the seeming lack of academic success among black youngsters as an adaptation to lower social and occupational positions as adults. In essence, Ogbu suggested "that the caste system imposes on blacks culturally constituted motives adaptive to their status positions," which undermined Ogbu's prior structural argument (Gould 1999, 176). Moreover, Gould (1999) outlined four components of the social structure that Ogbu missed in his analysis: real opportunity structures, cognitive expectations that emerge in adaption to opportunity structure, normative expectations, and the nature of the culture. The value commitments of inner-city people, including black people, were in line with mainstream values, Gould (1999) contended, and the cognitive expectations created as a result of opportunity structures are both accurate and functional.

Washington v. Davis

The implications of dismissing or minimizing the centrality of race in American society are massive. One example is evidenced in the 1976 *Washington v. Davis* case (Haney López 2000). The historic case has had a long-lasting impact on American society. In many ways, the case ignored the importance of a racialized social structure in producing racial disparities. The case involved a lawsuit brought against a police department in Washington, DC. To become a police officer in Washington, DC, applicants had to participate in a seventeen-week physical training, meet certain character standards, complete high school or equivalency, and score at least 40 out of 80 on a written exam. The court ruled that laws or procedures that do more harm to one group than they do to others, but on the surface were race neutral and did not directly intend to discriminate any group, were valid under the equal protection clause of the Fourteenth Amendment. The fact that a law or policy, in this case, application, to become police officers in the nation's capital had a disproportionate effect on black applicants was not enough evidence. This is particularly interesting given that many scholars, as mentioned earlier, point precisely to racial disparities in many social institutions as evidence of discrimination by the government, individuals, and so on. The ruling, in this case, implied that race had nothing to do with the process despite different outcomes by race. Moreover, the ruling also highlighted the court's lack of understanding about what racial discrimination looks like and how laws, policies, and procedures can on the surface appear race neutral but discriminate.

Although four times as many black people failed the required Test 21 as did white test takers is not in and of itself proof that the test is meant to keep black people off of the police force, claimed the court in the *Washington v. Davis* case. The plaintiffs argued the test had nothing to do with the job performance of officers and that there was no evidence the test in any way predicted success on the job. Some scholars have noted that the court has a habit of not asking the right questions. Angela Onwuachi-Willig (2019) made this point in her article about the connection between the *Washington* case and the *Loving v. Virginia* case. The *Loving* case challenged longstanding laws against miscegenation. The court in the *Washington* case did not ask important questions about the department's actions and whether they made sense given the purpose of the test. Instead, Onwuachi-Willig said the "Court essentially assumed the good faith in hiring a diverse police staff on behalf of the police department" (2019, 314). Moreover, "the Court blindly accepted the Department's claim that it was actively engaged in efforts to become a more diverse police force," or what Onwuachi-Willig aptly called the "we're trying" defense (2019, 314).

The court also implied that even the increased presence of black people in the department would somehow diminish the occupation, much like beliefs that the very presence of black people in all-white neighborhoods and schools, for example, would somehow ruin the institutions and the association of both as white space. The court said, regarding the elimination of the test, the police department "should not be required on this showing to lower standards or to abandon efforts to achieve excellence." Adding to the opinion of the court, Associate Justice John P. Stevens stated that the distinction between discriminatory purpose and impact was not as obvious as some may think. Conversely, Justice Brennan, writing the dissent along with Justice Marshall, said the decision could lessen the effectiveness of measures to safeguard against discrimination. As has been the history of the nation, the burden was unduly placed on the historically marginalized group to prove intent (Sullivan 1981). The court in the *Davis* decision offered an "extremely narrow meaning of the word intent" (Onwuachi-Willig 2019).

The court behaved in a way that members of the dominant racial group in America have acted in the past when confronted with issues about inequality and race. The court chose to ignore the facts. Historically, the court and members of the dominant racial group, more broadly, have chosen to ignore facts about the unequal treatment black people receive that don't fit their version of history or dominant narrative. Their version of history provides an orientation in the world for them. It justifies the privileges and benefits they continue to receive without any accountability and responsibility for the harms they may cause.

Takao Ozawa v. United States

Again, the court, speaking in one voice, did and said what the court had done in the past. For example, consider the case *Takao Ozawa v. United States* (1922). Ozawa was born in Japan and lived in the United States for two decades. He sued the United States because he wanted to become a citizen under the Nationalization Act of 1906. However, the act stated that only free white persons and persons of African ancestry could naturalize. Ozawa argued that Japanese people were white. He lost the case. A year later, Bhagat Singh Thind, a man of Indian ancestry, filed a petition for naturalization using some of the very language the justices used in the *Ozawa* case to disqualify his petition. Thind lost his case too. The court ignored the very facts it presented in the *Ozawa* case and justified doing so based upon the perspective of the so-called *common man*. Whiteness was what the common white man and white woman defined it. Neither Ozawa nor Thind were considered by white people as white, no matter what the science of the day claimed. In the *Washington v. Davis* (1976) case, as in the cases of *Ozawa* and *Thind*, the courts dismissed facts in evidence to rationalize the unequal treatment of nonwhite people in the country.

Whiteness and the Myth of a Postracial Society

Placing the burden on racial and ethnic minorities to prove their oppression and the source(s) of their oppression is an important element of whiteness. This is not only an important element, but I would consider it central to the maintenance of whiteness. It seeks to dismiss the idea that throughout much of American history white people have been beneficiaries of a system that negatively impacts people of color, particularly black people. Efforts to protect such a mischaracterization of whiteness are effective, so much so that historically, and continuing into the present, scholars, including black and white scholars, have retreated from advancing and promoting research that shows how the racialized social structure produces and reproduces inequalities by race. Additionally, some elected officials have embraced and introduced public policies that avoid addressing the structural factors underpinning racial phenomena.

Efforts to expose the continuing significance of race are often met with a great deal of what can best be described as white rage (Finley, Gray, and Martin 2020). For example, members of the dominant group have responded to claims of black disadvantage and unequal treatment with what some have described as religious fervor (Finley, Gray, and Martin 2020). They hope to drown out any voices that might be brave enough to speak out against ongoing racial injustices, including professional athletes like former San Francisco 49ers quarterback Colin Kaepernick and his supporters (Martin 2018).

Let us now turn our attention to some of the research on whiteness to better understand what the term means and how I apply it in *America in Denial: How Race-Neutral Policies Reinforce Racial Inequality in America*. Then, we will examine how members of the dominant racial group have succeeded in muting, or drowning out, the voices of those with opposing viewpoints.

While many contemporary scholars are only beginning to explore whiteness as a way of understanding why racial differences persist in America, people like W. E. B. Du Bois ([1921] 1975) were thinking and writing about whiteness in the early part of the twentieth century. In chapter 2 of *Darkwater: Voices Within the Veil*, Du Bois described the origins of what he called personal whiteness. Du Bois wrote that personal whiteness was a relatively recent phenomenon. Personal whiteness, for Du Bois emerged in the nineteenth and twentieth centuries. He described the onset as occurring relatively quickly. Du Bois wrote, "The world in a sudden, emotional conversation has discovered that it is white and by that token, wonderful" ([1921] 1975, 30). Through the idea that "whiteness is the ownership of the earth," came this "new religion of whiteness" (Du Bois [1921] 1975, 31–32).

For Du Bois, white people from diverse backgrounds consolidated around whiteness. There was a universal pride among white people that Du Bois argued back then could be seen in "the strut of the Southerners, the arrogance of the Englishman amuck, the whoop of the hoodlum" ([1921] 1975, 31). Du Bois declared, "The title to the universe claimed by white folk is faulty" ([1921] 1975, 31). The normalization and privileging of whiteness made members of the dominant group and others believe the myth "that every great soul the world ever saw was a white man's soul; that every great thought the world ever knew was a white man's thought; that every great deed the world ever did was a white man's deed; that every great dream ever sang was a white man's dream" (Du Bois [1921] 1975, 31).

Centering whiteness was purposeful, argued Du Bois ([1921] 1975). What Du Bois described first as comedy, and later tragedy, became particularly salient when nonwhites, but especially black people, insisted on the recognition of their human and civil rights. Resistance to antiblack sentiments led to the consolidation of white people from philanthropists and white Northerners who turned their backs on black people in the North and declared "that the South is right" (Du Bois [1921] 1975, 32). The consolidation of whiteness manifested itself (and still does) in sometimes violent ways from which neither black man, black woman, or black child could escape. Du Bois described this fervor as "drunk and furious with ungovernable lust of blood; mad with murder, destroying, killing, and cursing; torturing human beings because somebody accused of crime happened to be the same color as the mob's innocent victims and because that color was not white" ([1921] 1975, 33).

Whiteness has historically conceptualized black people as dark in skin color but also in the mind. Thus, the contention held by many people in the dominant racial group that "everything great, good, efficient, fair, and honorable is white . . . and the devil is black" (Du Bois [1921] 1975, 44).

Many scholars have drawn upon the work of Du Bois ([1921] 1975) on whiteness, in whole, or in part, to address the marginalization of important voices, including the voices of black women. The critique of whiteness, and the privileges associated with it, is considered an important stage in the study of whiteness. Indeed, the latest, or third wave of whiteness studies appears to claim Du Bois as one of its chief founders

(Twine and Gallagher 2008). However, one of the key characteristics of the latest wave of whiteness studies is the claim that not all white people are beneficiaries (Twine and Gallagher 2008). Claims of Du Bois ([1921] 1975) as a founder notwithstanding, this view of whiteness represents a departure from Du Bois and his work on whiteness. Du Bois clearly saw racial imperialism as critical to understanding the United States and the global society and his discussions about capitalism often addressed its impact on black people and other people of color throughout the world to the near exclusion of the white worker. On the contrary, Du Bois frequently addressed the implications of antiblack sentiments by white working-class folks toward black workers, and black people more broadly.

More recent studies about whiteness in sociology are considering how the development of an integrated approach to studying race and ethnicity might combat white supremacy and finally end the debate about what matters more, structure or culture. Zulema Valdez and Tanya Golash-Boza (2017) offered an intersectionality of race and ethnicity approach. The scholars argued that race and ethnicity are not the same but often revert to such claims in their work. Valdez and Golash-Boza (2017) also made the argument that an intersectionality approach to race and ethnicity will explain more about enduring divides and be more nuanced than other approaches. I note that Valdez and Golash-Boza (2017) did not specify how this might be accomplished. They also did not show specific flaws in existing studies, which they contend do not explain very much and are not nuanced at all. Furthermore, Valdez and Golash-Boza (2017) asserted that it is important to build a bridge between race and ethnicity scholars. The scholars did not give careful thought or consideration to whether scholars at either end of the race/ethnicity spectrum felt the need for a bridge. Moreover, Valdez and Golash-Boza's (2017) use of the term intersectionality in their article is problematic. Unfortunately, the term intersectionality is often misused. In this case, what Valdez and Golash-Boza (2017) were calling an intersectional approach was more like what W. Carson Byrd (2017) called an integrative approach.

It is important to note that intersectionality and integration are not the same things. It is also important to note Valdez and Golash-Boza's (2017) preferred approach will not end whiteness, or white supremacy, but instead may succeed in reifying both. George Yancy's (2000) article about feminism as a subtext of whiteness is illustrative of how this happens. In integrating two entities there is an underlying assumption that one group is moving from the margins only to join another group in part because that group has hoarded all the valued resources (i.e., power, property, prestige). Minority groups may be closer in physical proximity to the dominant group but continue to be far away politically and economically, for example. Integration often brings with it an illusion of inclusion, which would be the case in an integrative approach to combating whiteness.

The proposed integrative approach is a veiled attempt by ethnicity scholars to gain greater legitimacy and relevance harkening back to a time when the ethnic paradigm was dominant and studies about race and understanding new technologies of whiteness were marginalized (Gray, Finley, and Martin 2019). Zulema Valdez and Tanya Golash-Boza (2017) want to use the concept of a racialized social system as a connector between race and ethnicity scholarship when the concept is already commonly accepted and widely used in studies about race. Ethnic studies would benefit from such a move.

Perhaps the use of the term "ethnoraciality" is most telling about what an integrative approach to combating whiteness through sociological studies about race and ethnicity is really about—the erasure of race, particularly antiblackness, as central and foundational to understanding whiteness historically and in contemporary times. The term and the proposed integrative approach serve to minimize and obfuscate race. Valdez and Golash-Boza's (2017) approach is essentially a race-neutral or race-fair approach to studying that is doomed from the start.

Again, Yancy's (2000) work on whiteness and feminism is important here. The proposed integrative theory will, like whiteness in feminism, marginalize the voices and political concerns about race, especially black people in the United States. Similar to feminism as a subtext to whiteness, ethnicity as a subtext to whiteness "assumes to speak with universal authority and truth" (Yancy 2000, 156). Moreover, the suggested integrative approach to combating whiteness "assumes to think and to speak for the entire world" (Yancy 2000, 157). This " 'transcontexualized' conception of experience . . . is philosophically bankrupt and dismissive of particular experiences" (Yancy 2000, 157). No one group, or approach, "possesses the theory or methodology that allows it to discover the absolute 'truth' or, worse yet, proclaim its theories and methodologies as the universal norm evaluating other groups' experiences" (Yancy 2000, 165).

It is not a coincidence that when practices that are associated with antiblackness are extended to and experienced by other nonwhites, questions arise about whether the group represents the "new n****er," or the "new folk devil." Race matters. Race trumps ethnicity. Race-neutral and race-fair approaches to addressing whiteness and the resulting racial disparities only serve to buttress antiblack, anti-nonwhite sentiments.

There are many reasons that some scholars and elected officials, including some black scholars and elected officials, have gravitated more toward the idea that race-neutral and race-fair policies and scholarship are possible and necessary. For one, the backlash experienced by black scholars who dared confront whiteness in their classrooms, in their research, and in public, particularly on various social media platforms, has resulted in these scholars finding themselves the subject of virtual mobs with little protection from the administrators for whom they work (Finley, Gray, and Martin 2018).

Several recent events highlight how antiblack sentiments continue to frame the experiences of people in the United States whether they identify as black or not. The election of President Obama is an oft-cited example. It's not a coincidence that the number of hate crimes against black people increased during President Obama's tenure (Bigg 2008). The antiblack sentiment aimed at Obama and other black people led to the passage of seemingly race-neutral programs and policies with the exception of the My Brother's Keeper program. However, the program was designed in such a way that it did more to promote than undermine dominant narratives about young black men as deviant. The Obama administration missed many opportunities to directly address racial disparities in America.

For example, the Great Recession harmed black people in ways it did not harm others, due in large part to the fact that before the Great Recession black people were experiencing higher rates of unemployment, predatory lending practices, insecure employment, among other challenges, than white people. Despite the evidence of racial disparities before and after the Great Recession, programs to save the nation from what many people considered certain economic doom were not at all race specific. Some of the programs that were part of the recovery efforts passed during and after the Great Recession enhanced the policing and hypersurveillance of black people. Some banks and financial institutions were deemed too big to fail and received financial assistance as part of recovery efforts. The loss of black wealth, which was already dismal before the Great Recession, was not considered important by the Obama administration and nothing was done specifically for black asset owners.

Not wanting to fan the flames of antiblack sentiments is part of the reason that then presidential candidate Barack Obama chose Joe Biden as a running mate. Many Americans did not think the country was ready for a black president. Surely, the country was not ready for people from historically disadvantaged groups at the top of the Democrat ticket. However, Biden should have been considered a problematic choice for several reasons. For instance, Biden, a former opponent of Obama, once described Obama as *clean* and *articulate*. These terms are coded terms about the intelligence and cleanliness of black people more broadly. Also, Obama chose a man as his running mate who admittedly collaborated with segregationists and revictimized Anita Hill, who alleged sexual harassment by Clarence Thomas.

Another example of President Obama's failure to directly address race in substantive ways involved noted black scholar Henry Louis Gates. This example also points to the role of Biden to mute Obama's race. In July 2009, Gates was arrested after a confrontation with a white officer after someone called police claiming he was breaking into a home. The home belonged to Gates. Commenting on the arrest of one of the most respected scholars in the country, President Obama said the officer acted stupidly. Many white Americans swiftly rebuked Obama's comments. In America, the police are considered gods and Obama's criticism of the officer was viewed as a criticism of all police officers and of the whiteness police departments represent more broadly (Gray and Finley 2015). His words were considered sacrilegious. The message at the center of the rebuke of Obama's comments was clear—whiteness is always right and blackness is always a potential, perceived, or actual threat. Obama's solution to this racial issue was to hold a beer summit for those involved. Joe Biden, representing whiteness in the administration, attended the beer summit with the arresting white officer, Gates, and the president.

Responses to public protests about unnatural black deaths are also responsible for a shift toward race-neutral or race-fair policies, proposals, and research. Reactions to protests by Kaepernick and protests under the Black Lives Matter umbrella are two examples. What happens when an elite black athlete playing in a professional league that is governed by majority white CEOs and supported primarily by a historically white male fan base decides to use his status to draw attention to racial inequalities in America by kneeling instead of standing during the playing of the national anthem? Like many athlete-activists before him, Colin Kaepernick could not find work and there was an even broader backlash.

In response to the protests, restaurant owners who normally rely on sports fans as patrons refused to show National Football League (NFL) games. Fans, mostly white, demanded refunds from their cable providers.

Even President Trump got involved. The president insulted the players and their mothers on social media. President Trump also criticized the CEOs for not exerting more control over the players. Many white people boycotted Nike for supporting Kaepernick's right to protest. Nike stood behind Kaepernick again when the sneaker giant discontinued a shoe bearing the 1776 version of the American flag. Some people protested the design because that time period did not have the same meaning for everyone. While white people were celebrating their independence, black people were still in physical bondage.

Responses to protests by individuals and groups directly and indirectly associated with the #Black Lives Matter movement are another example of how whiteness consolidates when threatened. The killing of young Trayvon Martin sparked the onset of what some have described as a movement. The killing a few years later of Alton Sterling exposed further tensions between law enforcement and the black community. It was then that declarations that All Lives Matter and Blue Lives Matter most reached their zenith. In Baton Rouge, the site of Sterling's killing, blue ribbons went up on mailboxes and on houses in predominately white neighborhoods. Black and blue flags signifying solidarity with the police flew in the backs of trucks or were converted to magnets and stickers to adorn cars and trucks, including police vehicles, which are purchased with public funds. White runners in races from 5ks to half marathons ran the distance supporting law enforcement. In fact, legislators succeeded in passing a Blue Lives Matter law, making officers a protected class along with groups whose ancestors experienced enslavement, exclusion, segregation, expulsion, and near extermination.

It is no wonder that some individuals are retreating from the fight for the ongoing black liberation struggle, but the dangers of this trend continuing may have consequences for generations to come. Relative silence by some during the confirmation of Justice Clarence Thomas, for example, has impacted court decisions, including those impacting people of color for decades. Failure to place pressure on President Obama and others to introduce and administer race-specific initiatives was met with worsening conditions for many people of African ancestry in the United States, where such indicators as asset ownership, education, and contact with the criminal justice system are concerned. Fear of taking on more conservative theses, such as those put forth by Moynihan (1965) and others, has negatively impacted the scholarly and public discourse around issues of race, particularly as they relate to antiblack sentiments and related outcomes. The unwillingness on the part of some scholars and elected officials, among others, has emboldened some members of the majority group in America and their ability to control narratives, agendas, and mainstream media has not only placed black people at risk but also compromised the values and beliefs many in America claim to hold so dear.

America in Denial examines the myth of a race-fair America by exploring the danger (and the potential for additional harm) of universal programs and other race-neutral initiatives related to asset building, education, and criminal justice.

America in Denial is both important and timely. The belief that America is moving more toward a colorblind society is likely growing and the next phase of that perspective is the idea of a race-fair America. Many people with influence and power, from political candidates to local elected officials to scholars, are promoting race-neutral policies. The (mis) use of black scholars, in particular, provides cover for elected officials and presidential hopefuls needed to garner support and authenticity required to increase public support for their initiatives. There is a need to unpack and debunk these issues and there is a need to place them in appropriate historical contexts. Alternatives to potentially harmful universal, race-neutral policies and programs must be part of the conversation. *America in Denial* is expected to generate such conversations and related scholarship.

In chapter 1, "The Road to a Race-Fair America: How America Lost Its Way," I explore the rise of colorblind rhetoric as a means to downplay the role of race in America. In this chapter I also address the ways in which factors other than race, such as class, have been used in an attempt to debunk the idea that race is still the most significant determinant for black people in America.

"Wealth, Inclusivity, and Exclusion," chapter 2, examines racial disparities in the types and levels of assets owned. The causes and consequences of persistent racial wealth disparities and black asset poverty are discussed. A review of popular programs aimed at addressing the racial wealth gap are reviewed with special attention devoted to Individual Development Accounts (IDA), baby bonds, and reparations. I show how universal programs do not go far enough to address the racial wealth gap and will surely not lead to a race-fair America. Contributions from largely public sources are relatively small and come with a number of strings attached. Funds may only be used in limited ways, such as for the purchase of a home or for a business venture, for example. The programs ignore the relatively low returns on investments that black people receive from such assets when compared with white people in America. Previous research related to topics such as racial capitalism, philanthrocapitalism, and financial instruments as technologies of antiblackness are also reviewed and analyzed here. They inform the ways in which the programs identified may be understood as paternalistic and reflect a hypersurveillance of black bodies through such things as state-sponsored biometric registries.

Chapter 3, "From Compulsory Education to Universal Disappointment," describes how many Americans still view education as the great equalizer. Little has changed since the landmark *Brown v. Board of Education of Topeka, Kansas*, in that many schools are as segregated now as they were decades ago. Public schools, which are accessible to all, are often underresourced and feeders to what scholars have called the school-to-prison pipeline. Universal pre-K programs claim to benefit black people whose children have historically had limited access to such programs, relative to white people, but racial disparities are evidenced here as shown in initiatives aimed at addressing the educational challenges of black youths from the cradle through college. In this chapter I also review literature that underestimates the impact of the linkages between educational attainment, race, and the wealth gap. I address a number of recent trends that further exacerbate problems, including programs that call for universal community college, or college for all. These trends include historical declines in enrollment of black students and the dismal numbers of black graduate students and faculty. Claims of commitments to and the value of diversity notwithstanding, education, including universal and/or race-neutral policies and programs is not the only way, or even the best way, to a race-fair America.

In chapter 4, "The Color of Justice," I show how racial disparities in the criminal justice system are apparent from decisions about policing strategies to arrests to prosecutions. Nevertheless, programs and policies aimed at addressing violent crimes, curbing gang activities, and addressing quality of life issues are framed in such a way as to convince the public that they are race neutral and intended for the common good. Agents of the criminal justice system are also viewed as race neutral and thus virtually immune from criminal prosecution in cases, for example, involving a black civilian and a white police officer. Current policing strategies and criminal justice reforms aimed at addressing mass incarceration do not apply equally to all, nor are they experienced in the same way by all, and will not lead to a race-fair America.

Chapter 5, "Resistance and Racial Progress: Kaepernick and the Practice of Leadership," includes a discussion about what it looks like to fight back against race neutrality and the associated costs. Many members of the dominant group still believe that sports are purely for entertainment. Many decry athletes who decide to use their high profiles to bring attention to racial disparities in America, such as in the case of US Olympians in 1968 and National Football League (NFL) protests led by people such as Colin Kaepernick. I make the case that what is needed is more people like Kaepernick, who refused to wait for a more politically feasible time to draw attention to critical social problems.

In the conclusion, I outline what is required to get to a race-fair America. I address the potential challenges and ways to combat such affronts. I call upon white liberals to heed the warnings of people like the Reverend Dr. Martin Luther King Jr. I also call upon black scholars to revisit and embrace the scholarship and scholar-activism of people like W. E. B. Du Bois. I remind elected officials about what is needed and required of black leaders, including elected officials, by drawing from the works of black intellectual thinkers such as Malcolm X and Cornell West. The book concludes with a discussion about the danger of failing to speak truth to power out of fear and intimidation, including a discussion about racial disparities and the COVID-19 pandemic.

CHAPTER ONE

The Road to a Race-Fair America

How America Lost Its Way

Why are so many people afraid of white backlash? Fears about how white people from the president to ordinary white citizens may respond to statements, public policy initiatives, scholarly studies, social media posts, opinion pieces, and so on, addressing persistent racial inequalities and recommendations for redress, have had a tremendous impact on the quality of social discourse in America. White backlash is not a new issue, but the religious fervor with which it has been expressed over the past decade is noteworthy, as is the impact it has had on some of the most ardent fighters for social justice.

The actual and virtual mobs (Finley et al. 2018) that engage in a range of activities aimed at communicating disdain for nonwhite groups are terrorizing those with individual membership in these groups. Actual and virtual mobs are also paralyzing journalists, political pundits, and some academics, including black scholars. A purpose of these mobs is to strike fear in the hearts and minds of nonwhite people and anyone else who may want to join in the fight for social justice. Such mobs have historically been met with various forms of resistance from any number of interest holders.

The black press, for one, often provided a different perspective on accounts of such things as lynchings than the white mainstream press. White journalists were sometimes complicit in lynchings by failing to report certain facts or by misrepresenting facts about the perpetrators and the victims. Many black scholars and black elected officials were critical of the actions of mobs. Black scholars, black activists, and black elected officials called out the complicity of not only the white press but also white law enforcement officers, white elected officials, and white citizens who *saw* something but refused to *say* something.

Sadly, increasingly, these much-needed voices are either silent, silenced, or drowned out by the cries of individual white men and groups of mostly angry white men. Many of these angry white men say they long for a time, which few have actually identified, when America was great. Their dissatisfaction with where they think the country currently stands and what might happen if left unchecked has resulted in some black and white people claiming that little can be done to address persistent racial inequality. It has left many supporters thinking that it is not politically feasible to call for race-specific remedies. Instead, there are calls for programs and policies that are race fair and race neutral.

It is important to understand how so many people have arrived at what I consider to be a potentially very dangerous conclusion. The danger lies in the potential for exacerbating racial disparities at a time when black-white differences have already reached epidemic proportions, such as in the case of wealth inequality, criminal justice, and education. In order to understand how the nation might move beyond these enormous challenges, we must understand how we arrived at this place and time.

The answers, I argue, may be found in the origins of colorblind rhetoric and American civil religion. Colorblind white supremacy, according to Delgado (2018), can best be defined "as ideology, practice, and narrative that uses equality laden language to maintain systems of racism, white dominance, and white power" (541). Contrary to popular opinion, the idea of America as a colorblind nation did not begin with Dr. Martin Luther King Jr.'s famous "I Have a Dream Speech," as many scholars, journalist, and politicians have argued. Colorblind rhetoric originated with the birth of the nation. *Colorblind* rhetoric began with the creation of the nation's founding documents. The documents included language that rendered groups either visible or invisible, politically and metaphorically. The visible markers of race rendered some (white) Americans powerful, while rendering others, particularly black people, powerless. Whiteness was visible in the benefits and privileges afforded to white people and blackness, for example, was made invisible by the withholding of basic civil and human rights for people of African ancestry. Founders refused to *see* color by refusing to acknowledge the humanity and citizenship of black people.

Being seen and being visible meant having access to wealth, status, and power. In this way the founders and the sacred documents they created were color*blind* or blinded by color.

Colorblind rhetoric would later come to describe the co-opting of language related to values such as justice, fairness, and equality by white people in America to argue against race-based policies and programs aimed at addressing historical and contemporary discrimination against black people. The dominant narrative became that race-based policies and programs were not so cleverly veiled attempts by black people to discriminate against white people as retaliation for the individual and collective harm black people endured. Colorblind rhetoric has remained a part of the American lexicon and social fabric due in large part to the existence of what sociologist Robert Bellah called American civil religion in an article published in 1967. I will argue that American civil religion is an underutilized sociological concept that assists in our understanding of white backlash resulting from perceived black progress and fears of retribution. This is important for unpacking what appears to be dwindling support for race-specific programs to address current and past wrongs and the continued movement in support of race-fair and race-neutral initiatives that will do more harm to already outrageous racial disparities, particularly disparities between black and white people in America.

I will also argue that a misunderstanding of the difference between the politics of respectability and respectability politics is also partly responsible for the abandonment of efforts to push back against various forms of white backlash. The former focuses on fighting for social justice issues, controlling one's own image, and determining one's own fate, while the latter focuses on modeling the mythological values and standards of the white middle class in the hopes of achieving acceptance and economic parity with white people. Revisiting the origins of the politics of respectability can enhance our understanding of the critical difference between the two and about what is happening now and ways to overcome it. I begin with a brief discussion about color consciousness and colorblind rhetoric throughout American history. Color consciousness is a term I use here to refer to awareness and an acknowledgment of race and the role that it plays in the lives of people in America. For white people color consciousness may include a belief in white superiority and black inferiority and actions that support such claims and yield greater access to wealth, status, and power for individuals with membership.

Color Consciousness and
Colorblind Rhetoric in America

Many people today will say that they don't see color. The founding framers
of America did see color and they were blinded *to it* and *by it* as well.
They saw the color of white men as representing all that was right with the
world. They saw white men as worthy of privilege. They saw white men
as blessed by God and entrusted by God as partners in a divine plan for
the redemption of humanity. This divine plan, according to the founding
framers, not only included the expansion of the geopolitical territory of
the nation but also the domination of nonwhite people, most of whom
were not regarded as human beings; rather, they were regarded as subhuman, as animals, and as property. The use of the term *all* in founding
documents was both exclusive and inclusive. The term included all white
men, while simultaneously excluding Native Americans, Asians, Mexicans,
and people of African ancestry. The willingness to see whiteness and to
ascribe to it yielded a long list of benefits and privileges throughout the
periods both before and after the Civil War.

Indeed the American Revolution represented the gap between what
patriots said they valued and how they actually treated nonwhites. Patriots rallied around the idea that they were better than enslaved Africans,
for example, and should not tolerate being treated in such a way by the
British Empire. Their cry for freedom was in many ways recognition of
the illegitimate treatment of kidnapped and enslaved Africans at the same
time that it was a reification of whiteness as property, purity, and priest-
liness. They did not believe that white Americans should be subjected
to rule by a foreign power. They did not think they should be obligated
to a foreign government without sufficient representations. As colonies,
they were owned and, in many ways, dependent upon the crown. White
Americans sought to sever their ties and gain their independence, while
preserving the institution of slavery. White Americans were perfectly fine
with owning kidnapped Africans but did not want to be treated like them.

From the early decades of the 1600s through the end of the Civil
War, a number of laws were in place to reinforce the color-based hierarchy
of the nation—one where color was both visible and invisible. Whiteness
was visible and white privilege abounded, while blackness was rendered
as invisible because black people were essentially regarded as nonentities.
For example, laws were passed to determine the status of children born to
enslaved women. No such rules were necessary for white women. A child

born to an enslaved woman, however, was deemed the property of the enslaved woman's owner. In other words, the status of the child followed the status of the mother. The kidnapped African mother had no agency. She had no control over what happened to her child. She was treated as irrelevant and the child was regarded as just another asset in the owner's portfolio. White people were colorblind to the extent that they only saw the humanity in themselves despite their horrific treatment of others.

Color-conscious policies also determined who was fit to serve in military conflicts. Whiteness was to represent intelligence, loyalty, and bravery, which white people claimed black people, despite their participation in various military conflicts, did not possess and could not acquire. In this way, whiteness is seen and blackness is again rendered invisible. At the same time, white people were fearful that black people might enact revenge against them for all black people had endured. White Americans at the time were very conscious that their color might make them the targets of black people, and other historically disadvantaged colors, but at the same time failed to see the ways in which their obsession with othering was responsible for the relatively disadvantaged position of black people and the basis for the inhumane acts they experienced. The only color that mattered was whiteness and white people learned not to see how color matters in the experiences of black people and other historically marginalized groups, although in significantly different ways. While Asian, black, Hispanic, and even white ethnic groups experienced prejudice and discrimination from the racial majority group, their experiences were different and resulted in different outcomes. For example, white ethnic groups faced prejudice and discrimination in terms of housing and employment but were eventually aided in the assimilation process through the educational system and through access to home ownership and suburbanization, which accounts for their relative successes despite facing many challenges. The perpetuation of what Bellah called American civil religion was the driving force behind the unification of white people from different religious, class, and ethnic backgrounds against black people and against the world.

American Civil Religion

American civil religion exists alongside other religions, Bellah wrote in his 1967 article on the subject. He defined American civil religion as beliefs, rituals, and symbols of religious orientation that a majority of Americans share. Building upon Jean-Jacques Rousseau's *The Social Contract*, American civil religion includes the recognition of the existence of God, awareness of life to come, positive rewards of virtue and punishment for vice, and an exclusion of religious intolerance.

Rita Whillock defined American civil religion "as declarations of principles from competing groups seeking to define what America is and the values that should prevail" (1994, 375). Phillip Hammond observed, "Whenever national events are thought to be elements of some larger scheme which surpasses human design, we have at least the rudiments of civil religion" (1976, 171). American civil religion held that the United States was the primary agent of God's meaningful activity in history. America would shine as the primary society in terms of which individual Americans discovered personal and group identity and a community of righteousness (Hammond 1976).

Bellah (1967) did not specify white Americans, but there is enough evidence in the documents he considered important to the founding of American civil religion to support the idea that American civil religion referred primarily to white people, white Christians, specifically. For Bellah, American civil religion was derived from Christianity but was not the same. God was viewed as Unitarian, "related to order, law, and right" as opposed to salvation and love (Bellah 1967, 45). God was both involved and interested in American history. God, according to American civil religion, demonstrated a special concern for (white) America. "Egypt is Europe; America, the promised land" (Bellah 1967, 46). American civil religion "served as a genuine vehicle of national religious self-understanding" (Bellah 1967, 46).

Bellah analyzed historic documents and speeches to show evidence of the existence of American civil religion and the significance of American civil religion for the nation's leaders and inhabitants. He believed this was an effective methodological approach for an empirical analysis of American civil religion. Documents such as the Declaration of Independence and the inaugural addresses of past presidents, like John F. Kennedy, were examples and included themes and concepts that Bellah (1967) said were at the core of American civil religion. For example, a close reading of presidential documents and other artifacts revealed that God was the ultimate authority. God decided America was going to be great and that every American would have to sacrifice his or her individual wants, needs, and desires for that cause. Another example is the oath taken by every president. While the president takes an oath and declares his loyalty to the nation and to the people, he is ultimately responsible to God and God's plan for America.

Matthew Cloud (2004) wrote about the Pledge of Allegiance and its connection to American civil religion. The pledge, along with religiously based oaths taken by the president and people testifying in court and serving on juries, has changed overtime to reify the relationship between God and the United States. For example, in 1954, the phrase "Under God" was added. "The 1954 addition of the phrase 'Under God' converted the pledge from what had been an affirmation of future allegiance to the Republic into an affirmation of religious belief that the nation is 'Under God' and was founded 'Under God'" (Cloud 2004, 329).

According to American civil religion, God's plan for America is that it not only prosper but also lead the world. To be clear, for Bellah, "American civil religion is not the workshop of the American nation but an understanding of the American experience in light of the ultimate and universal reality; the reorganization entailed by such a new situation need not disrupt the American civil religion's continuity" (1967, 52). While American civil religion was firmly established as part of American society, there were moments, argued Bellah, when efforts were needed to reshape, reframe, and reimagine American civil religion. Specifically, Bellah observed that there were a number of times in American history whereby American civil religion faced what he called three trials. The first time occurred around the time of the American Revolution and focused on independence. The second took place at the time of the Civil War and focused on sacrifice, death, and rebirth. The third trial was marked by the turbulent 1960s and had to tackle "the problem of responsible action in a revolutionary world" (1967, 52). A fourth trial, I and others observe, occurred with the historic terrorist attack that occurred on American soil on September 11, 2001. The main issues were vigilance, militarization, and patriotism. American civil religion called upon Americans to say something if they saw something to prevent similar attacks. The fourth trial linked relinquishing certain personal rights, including some rights to privacy, for national security. Anyone questioning such calls was deemed unpatriotic. The very name of the act, the Patriot Act, passed shortly after the attack that killed more than three thousand people, is reflective of the focus on vigilance, militarization, and patriotism.

The United States recently experienced what Bellah (1967) might consider a fifth trial. It could be said that the fifth trial began with the Great Recession and the election of President Barack Obama. The fifth trial focused on redemption, specifically, the redemption of whiteness at home and abroad.

The Great Recession, which began toward the end of 2007 and lasted until about the middle of 2009, impacted large and small financial institutions. The economic downturn also impacted businesses that employed workers in many areas of the labor force. Many homeowners lost their homes to foreclosure. The United States experienced the equivalence of a historic hurricane followed by damaging flooding from residual rain. While economic packages were created to save financial institutions considered too big to fail, ordinary Americans with wealth saw their portfolios decrease in value.

Despite the fact that black people lost relatively more than other groups as a result of the Great Recession, they bore the brunt of the blame for it. Black people played a big role in the bursting of the housing bubble, some claimed. As in the past, when America experiences an economic crisis, black people are often scapegoated, and the effect of economic downturns on them, due in large part to their already disadvantaged starting point, is ignored or minimized. One need only look at the racial disparities in the impact of COVID-19 on black people relative to other groups. I address this in greater detail in the conclusion and in my description of a sixth trial in the history of American civil religion.

A great majority of Americans sought redemption not only economically but also redemption of their place as a world power, unreachable by threats beyond its borders, especially from so-called rogue nations and other entities long considered inferior to the United States. The fifth trial also required a focus on the consolidation of whiteness and redemption of whiteness that involves reiterating who is American. This included restricting access to the United States by nonwhite people and finding other ways to make America great again.

The birther movement was one example of reiterating who is American. During the fifth trial Obama's birthplace was questioned in part because he symbolized what a great many white Americans considered un-American. Donald Trump was one of the most recognizable and most vocal adherents of the birther movement. As many people well know, President Obama was born in Hawaii to a white mother raised in Kansas and his father was black and born in the country of Kenya. Obama spent some time traveling the world, including stays in Asia. Trump and others used this information to create a narrative of Obama as an outsider and as un-American. There were also claims that Obama was Muslim. For many white Americans Muslims, including Muslims who are black and Muslims from other racial groups, were not real Americans. Bias attacks on individuals who were perceived to be Muslim or of Middle Eastern descent in the wake of September 11th were prevalent.

Furthermore, Obama's mixed heritage was another example of his un-Americanness. For much of the nation's history, the mixing of races through sexual contact was unlawful and Obama was an example of some people's worst fears. Moreover, his electoral victory now meant that a man identifying racially as black would not only occupy the highest position in the land, and one of the most powerful positions in American civil religion, but he would also, at least in theory, be the face of the nation—and the face of the nation could never be black. Along came a candidate, Donald Trump, with plans to make America great again and redeem whiteness both in America and on the world stage.

Donald Trump's beliefs and behaviors about black people, women, and immigrants were not unknown to the people in the state where his empire is headquartered or throughout the country and the world. Long before Donald Trump considered running for president his name and reputation were solidified in popular culture. He was at the center of contests objectifying women. He took out a full-page ad in the *New York Times* to condemn to death a group of black and Hispanic teenagers accused of raping a white woman jogger in New York City's Central Park and to this day has refused to apologize for his actions or to acknowledge the innocence of the Central Park Five, despite the fact that all of the individuals have since been exonerated. Evidence has also pointed to a number of discrimination lawsuits against Trump and his enterprises, and to allegations that his companies have employed scores of undocumented workers. Such workers are one of the very groups Trump promised his supporters he would keep from coming into the country. Many white Americans have long felt that they had lost too many bouts with black people and other groups and were in need of redemption. Donald Trump was able to capitalize on this sentiment and continues to do so as what could be called the fifth trial continues.

As president, Obama was not only a target of efforts to reify American civil religion, he was also a chief priest of it. David Frank wrote about Obama's role in "recalling and rescuing the cosmopolitan expression of American civil religion" (2011, 605). The inclusion of a well-known black and white minister, Joseph Lowery and Rick Warren, during Obama's first inauguration was evidence of these expressions. The two clerics helped signal what Frank (2011) called Obama's cosmopolitan theology. Unlike other presidents, Obama did not separate his public and private religious self, argued Frank. Moreover, Obama's more cosmopolitan American civil religion did not identify with Moses but Joshua in that he distinguished himself from the old civil rights movement vanguard. Obama did "adopt a fatalistic explanation of African American trauma" (Frank 2011, 613). For me, this signals not only a cosmopolitan form of American civil religion but also a move toward embracing a more race-neutral view of the country and an unwillingness to fully embrace and redress the historical and contemporary experiences of black people in America in meaningful ways. "Obama places racial trauma in its historical context, views spiritual and constitutional interpretation as a 'conversation' yielding new insights, places his audience in its generational and temporal setting, and insights that this trauma can be 'worked through'" (Frank 2011, 613) but in race-neutral ways that lack effectiveness. Frank also made the claim that Obama attempted to rework myths about America's founding to include excluded groups: "Obama completed an outline of a cosmopolitan civil religion that can host religion and atheism, Christianity and Islam" (2011, 621).

A sixth trial has emerged due to the COVID-19 global pandemic and the key word here is LIBERATION. Much like the previous trials, there is a perception among members of the dominant racial group in America, most visibly, white men in America, that they are being victimized. Policies aimed at "flattening the curve" have been framed by white men from the president to several of his advisors to members of the Republican Party, particularly in states led by Democratic governors, as infringing upon *their* rights. Direct and implied calls for white men to protect and exert their rights, namely, those afforded by the First and Second Amendments, are troubling, but not surprising when understood within the context of American civil religion. The contemporary response to the perceived attack on America, read as white America, by way of state and federal stay-at-home orders aimed at slowing the spread of the COVID-19 global pandemic, was religious and American civil religion is a powerful analytical tool for informing the sociology of religion and public discourses about the roles of race and religion in society, including American civil religion.

The perceived inherent pathology of nonwhite bodies, especially black bodies, has resulted in the past in a failure to adequately respond to a social challenge. For example, sickle cell anemia impacts people of all races, but it is considered colloquially as a black disease (Ciribassi and Patil 2016) and has not received the attention and support that other diseases have received by way of a federal response over many administrations. Many have compared the response to the crack epidemic and the ongoing opioid epidemic. The former, which disproportionately impacted black people, resulted in the further criminalizing of an entire group of people, while the latter, which disproportionately impacts white people, was medicalized and showered with federal resources ("A Tale of Two Epidemics" n.d.).

The reverence showed to white bodies and matters impacting white people emboldens commonly held myths and stereotypes that are at the core of American civil religion and whiteness. Long before Theodore Roosevelt and the Rough Riders, there was a perception about the linkages between the body, the nation, and religion. Concepts such as Christian masculinity and muscular assimilation are noteworthy here (Martin 2017). This is to say that despite the numbers and what is still not known about COVID-19, some members of the dominant group believe that they are at greater risk of losing their rights as citizen than contacting COVID-19 and view "social distancing" strategies imminent threats.

The myth that COVID-19 or any other tragedy or trauma of the magnitude of a Hurricane Katrina or a COVID-19 pandemic does not discriminate is simply not true. However, myths and misrepresentations have their place in American civil religion and are key for explaining white responses in such moments. Their perceived victimization lies in a strong adherence to American civil religion and their perceived supremacy as both white individuals and as a nation.

During what I am calling a sixth trial, many members of the dominant group struggled to come to terms with the difference between how America, especially white America, sees itself and the reality of how America actually works. Many experienced *white religious shock*, a disorientation based upon their racial position as it became painfully clear that the nation was ill-prepared to deal with an issue of this magnitude. It was unfathomable, for many, for example, how a nation that has long viewed itself as the savior of the world did not have enough basic personal protective equipment (PPE) for healthcare officials or first responders, who are often worshiped as heroes or treated as gods. It was likely incomprehensible to many that the nation lacked an adequate number of ventilators to support patients in need. The fact that the nation with the world's best and brightest had no reliable means of curing people of COVID-19 or vaccinating people against it was hard for some to grasp.

Without an effective way to test people for COVID-19 and no reliable cures available, many states announced disaster declarations and a national emergency, mentioned previously, was declared. A patchwork of plans meant that some states had very strict policies relative to others and, for a time, some states had no plans at all. According to the *New York Times*, by early April 2020 at least three hundred million people in about forty states were under some type of stay-at-home order. Washington, DC, for example, issued a stay-at-home order on March 30, 2020. Mayor Muriel Bowser said staying at home was the best way to "flatten the curve." Residents were instructed not to leave their homes unless they were engaged in essential activities, such as for medical appointments, buying food, performing or accessing essential governmental functions, and working at essential businesses. Failure to comply with the order could result in a fine of up to $5,000, imprisonment up to ninety days, or both.

In New York, nonessential businesses were closed as of March 22, 2020. Nonessential gatherings of individuals of any size for any reason were prohibited. Residents were asked to stay no less than six feet from others. Limitations were also placed on outdoor recreational activities. The maximum fine for violators was $1,000.

In Louisiana, as of March 11, 2020, nonessential businesses were to close. Residents were asked to exercise proper social distancing in public and all gatherings of ten people or more were prohibited. The order outlined examples of essential activities. No fines or imprisonment were mentioned.

Michigan announced a stay-at-home order that went into effect on March 24, 2020. Michigan's order prohibited nonessential in-person work and called for social distancing. Violation of the order was described as a misdemeanor.

Public service announcements featuring the chief executive officers of major corporations, college football coaches, entertainers, local elected officials and others encouraged people to do their part to mitigate the threat of COVID-19 by obeying the orders and staying home. While some people viewed the orders as necessary, others viewed them as a threat.

Media accounts of largely white people protesting in states, such as Michigan, are framed as protests against social distancing orders. *Daily Mail* published an article about COVID-19 protesters (Papenfuss 2020). White House advisor and member of a group calling themselves the "Save Our Country" coalition, Stephen Moore, reportedly compared the individuals who were in direct violation of Michigan's order, to civil rights icon Rosa Parks. Moore stated they were "protesting against injustices and lost liberties." Moore reportedly told another news outlet, "We need to be the Rosa Parks here, and protest against these government injustices." Moore is also a member of Trump's back-to-work council.

Mary Papenfuss (2020), the author of the *Daily Mail* article, described the protests as part of a "new onslaught against Democratic-led states fueled by the Trump campaign." Nicole Hemmer, a historian, was quoted in the Papenfuss (2020) article. The Columbia University–affiliated historian said the focus on "personal freedom" was actually an excuse for getting out and rallying against politicians they oppose. The lack of enforcement for violators of the protests have drawn comparisons to the military response to Black Lives Matter protests, which signals an immunity rooted in whiteness during the pandemic.

To further add fuel to the fire, Trump tweeted a message meant not only for the protesters but for his political base more broadly. He tweeted, "LIBERATE Michigan, Minnesota, and Virginia." In another tweet, he communicated more to his followers. On April 17, 2020, he tweeted, "LIBERATE Virginia and save your great 2nd Amendment. It is under siege. Additional protests were held following the tweets.

The protests in Michigan were organized by Michigan Conservative Coalition. The group is also known as Michigan Trump Republicans. The Michigan Freedom Fund, according to Papenfuss's (2020) article, promoted the protests. The group's official website states the group "fights to champion conservative policies on behalf of Michigan taxpayers." On the group's website it also states a commitment "to the principles of limited government, transparency in government, and the freedoms found in the Constitution." The Michigan Freedom Fund vows to "protect Freedom."

In addition to the protests in Michigan, there were other ways that largely white people resisted or pushed back against local, state, and national orders. Many white evangelicals continued to hold in-person services. In Louisiana, a COVID-19 hot spot, the Life Tabernacle Church defied the state and national stay-at-home order. The pastor, Tony Spell, held Easter Sunday services on April 12, 2020. About 1,300 people attended the service, according to Papenfuss (2020). The lawyer representing the pastor, Jeff Wittenbrink, eventually tested positive for COVID-19 and required hospitalization. Congregants in Kentucky and Florida also refused to comply with state and national measures to flatten the curve resulting in the arrest of at least one pastor (Mazzei 2020). Additionally, Liberty University in Lynchburg, Virginia, welcomed faculty, staff, and students back to campus as many colleges and universities transitioned to online instruction. By April 17, 2020, two employees and one student tested positive for COVID-19, reported Richmond.com.

While as many as eleven states included some form of exemptions for religious organizations, far too many complied with social distance recommended guidelines. *ABC News* described the issue as a constitutional issue. "Religious institutions are widely believed to be protected from such regulations by the concept of church and state protected in the First Amendment. But whether that is actually the case is unclear." In the past, the Supreme Court has held "that a law cannot 'unduly burden' a specific religion unless there is a 'compelling interest' in doing so, and that burden must be applied equally to secular institutions." Liz Alesse, author of the *ABC News* article "With Constitutional Questions Murky, Some Churches Continue to Defy Restrictions on Gatherings," also reported that the burden may be more of an issue for some religious groups than others. Some Jewish and Amish groups are not able to stream services online due to restrictions related to the use of electricity. Moreover, some religious groups, such as certain sects of Judaism, require at least ten people in order to practice their religion. Alesse described this as a constitutional issue, "a tug-of-war . . . between some state and local governments over whether religious gatherings should be allowed while the coronavirus outbreak rages on."

Media accounts of the protests against stay-at-home orders and public discourse are missing very important points that American civil religion can explain. The key issues here are not chiefly about constitutional rights but a perceived threat against whiteness. Consequently, many members of the dominant group are rallying around the president's call for LIBERATION in defiance of his own administration's directives. The president is showing, as he has done in the past, a keen ability to tap into the fears of many people who fear that their perceived superior position at home and abroad is under attack. The fears run counter to the promises embedded in American civil religion. The fervent response to such perceived attacks on whiteness is best understood as a religious. Whiteness is religious. Whiteness demands consolidation across various social and demographic groups.

In order to more completely comprehend the white backlash directed at social distancing measures, it is important that scholars, the media, and the general public broaden our understanding of religion. Religion is not simply a social institution as it is commonly treated in the scholarly literature or in the popular press. The late religious scholar Charles Long

(1999) provided an appropriate definition. Long defined religion as an "orientation in the ultimate sense, that is, how one comes to terms with the ultimate significance of one's place in the world" (1999, 7). He described religion as "more than a structure of thought; it is experience, expression, motivation, intentions, behaviors, styles, and rhythms" (1999, 7).

Decades earlier, Du Bois described the religion of whiteness, as noted earlier (Du Bois 1995). "Long before the recent discourse on critical race theory and critical white studies, Du Bois called into question white superiority and white privilege, and the possibility of white racelessness and/or white racial neutrality and universality. He was one of the first theorists to chart the changes in race relations from de jure to de facto forms of white supremacy" (Rabaka 2007, 2).

Finley and Martin (2017) extended discussions about whiteness as religious in their book chapter "The Complexity of Color and the Religion of Whiteness." The scholars described whiteness as a religious orientation as "a deep symbol that is connected in concrete ways to systems of unearned benefits in America, systems that deny others those same privileges" (Finley and Martin 2017, 180). Whiteness as a religious orientation "is the organizing principle of America, so deeply embedded in the structures that it functions as and through concealment" (Finley and Martin 2017, 180). James Perkinson (2004) agrees that whiteness is not only a racial category but a religious one as well. For Perkinson (2004), whiteness creates a subjectivity that is theological and functions as invisible and innocent. According to Finley and Martin:

> That whiteness is religious is, in part, what accounts for its durability and its ability to withstand deconstruction and dissolution. It is so ensconced in the structures that it often is misapprehended or, more often, invisible. . . . People with African heritage and heritage from other parts of the world, shall continue to find themselves on the outside of the religion of whiteness. . . . The religion of whiteness is exclusive. It is a closed system. (2017, 194)

Evidence of the religion of whiteness as a closed system is abundant and, I argue, is transmitted daily through the various functions of American civil religion. Grace Kao and Jerome Copulsky (2007) correctly pointed out that the "category of civil religion usually illuminates what is at stake in constitutional debates" (121). Instead of viewing the protests as threats to First and Second Amendment rights, among others, the defiant stance of predominately white people should be framed as "a dispute between contested meaning, significance, and propriety of civil religion in America itself" (Kao and Copulsky 2007, 121). Claims that the rights of Americans, read as namely white Americans, were being jeopardized highlights how civil religion "participates in the kind of 'sacred legitimation of the social order'" (Kao and Copulsky 2007, 132).

Kao and Copulsky (2007) identified four functions of American civil religion: preservationist, pluralist, priestly, and prophetic. Each is useful for unpacking protests against social distancing guidelines. The preservationist and pluralist perspectives represent the character of American civil religion, while the priestly and prophetic perspectives represent the contact, Kao and Copulsky (2007) argued. The preservationist perspective focuses on the ritual of claiming attacks on freedoms, such as the focus on liberation in the present uprising (Kao and Copulsky 2007).

The responses by white worker protesters was particularly representative of the preservationist perspective. This perspective includes "the continued use of traditional expressions, tropes, and rituals of civil religion is necessary to maintain cultural coherence, sense of national identity and the stability of our central institutions" (Kao and Copulsky 2007, 132). With this perspective, Kao and Copulsky (2007) observed that American equals Christian to the exclusion of other religious groups. I argue that in the COVID-19–related protests that American equals white. White backlash against the stay-at-home orders "accordingly find it appropriate for our symbolic systems to reflect and reinforce that identity" (Kao and Copulsky 2007, 132). Further evidence of these concerns on the part of protesters may be found in their gravitation toward the "Make America Great Again" mantra and the affiliation and support of coalitions, such as "Save Our Country." For the people openly defying the state and federal orders, protests demonstrate a belief in the exclusive access to basic and civil rights, as well as to material gain. Indeed, "the very heritage that such preservationists are striving to protest is itself a selective retrieval of certain events, symbolic memories, and interpretations—one that distorts or suppresses any evidence that does not conform to their desired image" (Kao and Copulsky 2007, 134). The preservationist protesters not only long for an unspecified time when America was great, they are "also willing to use such a vision to exclude or marginalize whomever is currently regarded as the . . . Other" (Kao and Copulsky 2007, 134).

Claims that everyone is essentially at equal risk for contracting the virus and related negative reactions to the protesters were reflective of the pluralist perspective. The pluralist or multicultural perspective proports to celebrate diversity and see it as a strength. Calls to stay home to do our part were indicative of such claims despite the fact that some groups were more at risk than other groups. Black people were overrepresented among COVID-19 deaths in selected cities. Additionally, preservationists expect assimilation, which creates a climate that is "very difficult for a self-consciously pluralist civil religion" to result in "a shared understanding of national identity and purpose" (Kao and Copulsky 2007, 138).

The priestly perspective is most related to the regard toward the state. It often involves legitimization of the state, institutions, and policies by infusing its rituals with religious grammar and employing the use of theological symbols. The priestly perspective also claims that support of the political order by the state is warranted. This perspective is not only shown in the expectations of the white worker protesters that the often democratically led states reverse course but also in the unwillingness to comply with the orders by religious leaders. It is important to note that while high-profile pastors openly defied the state and national orders, one of the largest predominately black churches, the Church of God in Christ (COGIC), responded in the opposite way. The leader of the COGIC urged its members not to hold large gatherings and called for a corporate prayer and fast on behalf of not only the United States but also countries impacted around the world (Blake 2020). The response from COGIC was not only reflective of the need to flatten the curve but also indicative of a keen awareness that responses for defiant black people would likely look very different than defiance by white people, white workers, white congregants, white college administrators, or white clergy. White clergy, in particular those leaders who received summons for violating orders, engaged in an age-old American civil religious practice. White clergy in defiance of the orders attempted to marry God with country in ways that justified their actions and reified their identity, not just as faith leaders but as (white) Americans. White clergy also attempted to give religious sanctity to what they viewed as patriotism. American civil religion provided the medium for merging or consolidating seemingly conflicting associations and loyalties to a religiously endowed loyalty (Finley, Gray, and Martin 2020).

The position taken by the white clergy and by white workers also revealed how American civil religion functions from the prophetic perspective. This perspective does not view the nation as the ultimate authority. Instead, the prophetic perspective observes that there is a higher authority than the nation. White worker protesters questioned the ultimate authority of their state governments, and to an extent of the national state, all the while receiving mixed messages from American civil religions' high priest, President Trump (Bellah 1967). The white workers and the white clergy leaders offer a self-criticism pointing to their vision of what the country needs to be. For them, the state has much more to focus on than whether they maintain six feet of distance from someone or whether they choose to attend worship services.

The COVID-19 global pandemic is already a defining event in human history from a social, demographic, and public health perspective. Responses to stay-at-home orders that resulted in protests in the street and in pulpits largely by white people highlight that the COVID-19 pandemic in America is also already a defining event in human history from a religious perspective. It is not enough to simply see the protests as a constitutional issue. It is imperative to view the protests as demonstrative of the religion of whiteness and how it functions according to American civil religion.

Bellah's (1967) original article on American civil religion has received criticism from many different disciplines. Some scholars have written that Bellah "exaggerated the unifying power of civil religion's rituals" (Hammond et al. 1994, 22), a perspective with which I disagree. Bellah's perspective on American civil religion was not "sensitive to clashing social values and to the forces of historical change" (Hammond et al. 1994, 23) and miscalculated "the ongoing interplay between civil religion and American culture as a whole" (Hammond et al. 1994, 23).

Jürgen Heideking (1994) disagreed with what Bellah (1967) identi-fied as the starting point of American civil religion. Heideking expressed surprise that Bellah did not point to earlier rituals and celebrations, which provided "the most concrete and highly visible efforts to establish a national civil religion" (1994, 369). This reconsideration of the starting point for American civil religion, said Heideking (1994), actually provides more support for Bellah's (1967) main ideas. Militias, fireworks, public readings of the Declaration of Independence, and patriot speeches pro-moted a sense of American identity, promoted economic self-confidence and belief in progress, and fostered an American consensus and national identity. These early rituals and celebrations ushered in a new political system, religious legitimacy, wedded to old symbols and rituals that gave them new meaning and a new ideology (Heideking 1994).

Michael Lienesch (2018) published an article called "Contesting Civil Religion," which also included a number of critiques about scholarship on American civil religion. Lienesch (2018) argued that Bellah (1967) failed to acknowledge that American civil religion was not only political but also cultural. Bellah (1967) also missed the fact that American civil religion was an "evolved tradition" (Lienesch 2018, 98). Moreover, the boundaries between civil and sectarian religion were more porous than Bellah explained. Lienesch (2018) said churches played important roles in American civil religion. Churches were indeed agents of American civil religion as evidenced by the decorum in many sanctuaries. It was not uncommon, for example, to see sanctuaries decorated with American flags and service banners honoring various branches of the US military (Lienesch 2018). American civil religion was more fluid than Bellah (1967) outlined. American civil religion, wrote Lienesch (2018), adapted and developed at various points over time, such as at the close of the 1920s. For example, "The Star-Spangled Banner" was adopted as the national anthem in 1931. New memorials, rituals, closing benedictions to presidential speeches, and the addition of "God Bless the United States of America" at the end of presidential addresses were other examples of adaptations and developments of American civil religion. According to Lienesch:

> In many variations, civil religion discourse has been embraced by both critics and friends of the New Deal in the 1930s and 1940s, by anticommunist crusaders and civil rights activists in the 1950s and 1960s, by culture warriors and antinuclear protesters in the 1980s, and by supporters and opponents by the "War on Terror" in the early twenty-first century. (2018, 116)

Debates about American civil religion grew to include multiple meanings (Lienesch 2018). Debates about new interpretations of American civil religion included nontheists' language (Weller 2013), among others.

M. Elaine Botha (1983) offered a criticism of civil religion more broadly. Writing about civil religion in South Africa, Botha cautions against labeling something civil religion. Botha wrote that "the mere presence of religious themes such as suffering, rebirth, destiny, calling, etc. might be indicative of the presence of civil religion traits, but need not necessarily point to ideological elements" (1983, 251). Herein lies what I consider a mischaracterization of King and others as spokespersons for American civil religion and even the existence of a black American civil religion.

Jana Weiss (2019) offered commentary on King and what he called the pitfalls of American civil religion. Weiss described conceptualizations of black people as a chosen people within a chosen people. "King evolved as an interpreter of a highly critical, African American civil religion influenced by the African American jeremiad" (2019, 435). Weiss added that American civil religion has done more harm than good to King's legacy. Linkages between American civil religion and King's legacy have "distorted and muted King's radical message of social change, rendering his call for political activism obsolete" (Weiss 2019, 447).

Another example of the misidentification of critiques of American society as reflective of some form of American civil religion is found in Randall Burkett's work on Marcus Garvey. Burkett (1978) described Garveyism as a religious movement that institutionalized a black civil religion. Garveyism "provided a common set of shared beliefs and value commitments which sought to bind its adherents—all those men and women of African descent who proudly took the name Negro—into a collectivity which was divinely called to a task in the world" (Burkett 1978, 67). Garvey was able to accomplish this, at least in part, by making sure people from separate denominations would participate in Universal Negro Improvement Association (UNIA) activities. Garvey used symbols, rituals, and beliefs that were rooted in their shared experience and built upon the shared experience of slavery and history of racial discrimination, interpreting it into

> the light of a transcendent goal: the uplift of the Negro race and the redemption of Africa. They stood as symbols of national solidarity, binding all men who willingly accepted the . . . term Negro into a single people whom God had specifically chosen for the task of building up a nation in Africa—a nation capable, first, of securing that continent's freedom and, second, of ensuring the rights of Negroes wherever they might reside in the world. (Burkett 1978, 67)

Tracey Hucks (2014) has written about religious nationalism, which more aptly described what people like King, Garvey, and others embodied. Specifically, Hucks outlined "forms of religious nationalism that mobilized around hermeneutical conceptions of Africa that affected religion, history, culture, style, language, and ideology" (2014, 8). Hucks revealed the various "ways African Americans sought to re-own or repossess Africa through textual reflection and religious expressions that centered Africa as the progenitor of a reestablished history" (2018, 8). They rejected the "socialized ontological deficiency" that was thrust upon them, while firmly believing in their own identity (Hucks 2014, 24). Embracing the beauty of blackness, even the idea that God was black, "is not only theologically defensible, but is a necessary corrective against the power of domination" (Hucks 2014, 24). Garvey, like King, was politically focused but also used religious and theological approaches in "rehumanizing pejorative impressions of blackness" (Hucks 2014, 24). Religious nationalism, argued Hucks, "redresses . . . historical problems of black moral essence, ontological heathenism, and spiritual pathology" (2014, 40). Religious nationalism, not American civil religion, or even a black American civil religion, facilitated both racial and religious agency with an emphasis on "the inner side of the color line" (Hucks 2014, 41). Religious nationalism provides African Americans with a space of transcendence by moving beyond politics, economics, and nationhood: "Its quest is often for a place of shelter from the political disenfranchisement, bodily invasion and assault, and socioeconomic and identity trauma visited upon people of African descent" (Hucks 2014, 45).

While Burkett (1978) was correct in his assessment that Garvey is misunderstood and the reasons why, namely, that he was often understood through the eyes of his critics, he mislabels Garveyism as a form of American civil religion when it is more accurately placed within the framework of religious nationalism.

Despite the criticisms, there seems to be no documented criticism of the idea that American civil religion actually endured three trials. This implies that American civil religion at various points in American history was at risk. I argue that what Bellah called trials, including the three I added, are better understood as *peaks of panic*. I draw upon the work of Derrick Bell (1992a) in making this claim. Bell (1992a) wrote on many subjects, including racial realism. Bell (1992a) reflected on the history of race in America. He wrote about historic periods where it seemed as though black people were making great strides toward becoming more included in American society. These periods included the end of physical bondage and various legislative victories. The legislative victories, such as the landmark *Brown* case, the Civil Rights Act of 1964, and the Voting Rights Act of 1965, were supposed to end the forced separation of black and white people in schools, in areas of public accommodation, and remove barriers to the ballot. Nevertheless, schools remained separate and unequal. Black people continued to face racial discrimination in many areas of public life, and access to the polls remained a challenge. Bell (19922) understood these historical moments as peaks of progress and not as fundamental changes that altered the racialized social structure that has characterized America for much of its history. Bell (1992a) argued for an understanding that the more things seemed to change, the more things really stayed the same and in some instances got worse. Embracing this reality, for Bell (1992a), would lead to an avoidance of feeling a sense of disappointment in the lack of actual progress on racial matters in America. Bell (1992a) assured those committed to social justice that there was satisfaction in the fight but reminded them that the outcome of then and future battles was already known. The powerful would only concede power so long as it was in their interest and in ways that would not alter the racial status quo.

We can think about Bellah's (1967) trials in a similar way. The perceived threats to whiteness, to American civil religion, were indeed just perceptions. The trials associated with the American Revolution, the Civil War, the modern civil rights movement, 9/11, the Great Recession, the election of President Obama, and protests over COVID-19 stay-at-home orders were merely periods of panic on the part of white people in America. They were moments of intense fear followed by overt acts of public rage, but they were by no means evidence of any threats to American civil religion.

Contemporary colorblind ideology is an important feature of American civil religion. Colorblind ideology serves to protest whiteness and promote a myth of inclusion while promoting exclusion. The contemporary origins of colorblind ideology are often traced back to Dr. Martin Luther King Jr.'s historic "I Have a Dream" speech, delivered at the March on Washington. The focus on a few lines from the speech is indicative of a methodological problem that befell Bellah's (1967) work on American civil religion. Bellah (1967) chose to focus on a few selected documents to substantiate the existence of an American civil religion. While American civil religion exists, support for its existence is not only found in the words of a few documents and speeches written and uttered by presidents, but more importantly it is supported by the actions of many individuals, some with legitimate governmental authority and others who have been deputized by virtue of being considered white. A few lines from King's speech have been used and misused in a similar way to support American civil religion and colorblind ideology. This is particularly clear when one examines the debates about the establishment of a holiday in King's honor.

North Carolina senator Jesse Helms claimed the holiday would be too expensive, costing the nation upward of $5 billion in lost wages. Helms also argued that King was a proven Marxist, and thus un-American and unworthy of a national holiday.

Arguably, the people of Arizona put up the most opposition to the King holiday (Alozie 1995). Arizona was the last state to approve the King holiday and the only state to bring the matter to a popular vote. In 1986 Governor Babbitt authorized a paid King holiday for state employees. Governor Mecham later rescinded the holiday. The state endured a boycott by the National Football League (NFL) for their refusal to honor the holiday. Commissioner Tagliabue moved the Super Bowl from Tempe, Arizona, in protest.

An examination of King's written and life's work beyond the speech show that while he hoped for a time in America's history where race would not be the determining factor in the life chances and life opportunities for anyone, especially for black people, that he favored race-specific solutions to race-specific problems. This is evidenced in King's support for black power.

Many historians and nonhistorians like to frame King and calls for black power as oppositional when in fact King had much to say about the value of promoting black power. While it is true that King did not favor the use of the term, he did not denounce the sentiment. King was far more concerned with how the white press and white Americans would misinterpret the meaning. King (1967) makes this clear in his book, *Where Do We Go from Here: Chaos or Community?*

In his book, King (1967) described how the phrase black power was introduced into the movement. King (1967) stated that the phrase was first used within the movement in Greenwood, Mississippi, during the James Meredith Freedom March. The march began with James Meredith and was continued by others following Meredith's near-death experience. Meredith was shot fighting for social justice issues. In *Where Do We Go from Here*, King (1967) assessed the values and what he saw as the liabilities of the term. King (1967) acknowledged that black power was a response to the misuse of white power. White power was degrading of black people and thus the term black power "had a ready appeal" (King 1967, 30). King understood that the utterance and meaning of the phrase black power aimed to "build racial pride and refute the notion that black is evil and ugly" (1967, 31). King (1967) highlighted some of the ways in which white power signaled that greater value was placed on the lives of white people than on the lives of black people, such as in the deaths of people connected to the movement. This was true in the ways that white public officials and the white press reacted to such deaths. King also expressed disappointment with white Christians who, he said, appeared "to be more white than Christian" (1967, 36).

King (1967) was not the one-dimensional symbol for race-neutral policies and programs framed as his legacy today. On the contrary, King understood that the root of the so-called Negro problem was not of his own making but was the result of an "indelible imprint of inferiority," which was the result of a history that "has been soiled by the filth of worthlessness" (1967, 39). King believed that one goal of black power was "to resurrect joyously the African past" (1967, 41). Like Bell (1992), and others, King (1967) was skeptical about just how meaningful legal decisions and legislation could be in changing the racial contours of American society. This is clear when he articulated, "No Lincolnian Emancipation Proclamation or Kennedyan or Johnsonian civil rights bill can totally bring this kind of freedom" (King 1967, 44). In essence, King (1967) was signaling the limit to which American civil religion could reach. In other words, it was not designed to extend to black people, and this is particularly important because a number of scholars have associated King (1967) not only with colorblind ideology but also with American civil religion.

To be clear, King (1967) was also critical black power. He did not agree that separatism, an idea some adherents to black power ideology embraced, was the answer to America's race problems. He thought separatism contained within it "seeds of its own doom" (King 1967, 45). He felt that alliances with the majority group were important, but over the course of his brief life he became increasingly skeptical about their effectiveness and sincerity.

Mary Frances Berry's work also showed that King did not endorse colorblind ideology. On the contrary, Berry stated that "civil rights advocates insisted that while color-blindness was a goal, remedies for discrimination could use race to get beyond the effects of racism against African Americans" (1996, 139). King and others were denounced when they advocated for change beyond neutrality, argued Berry (1996). They faced accusations that focusing on group discrimination violated American individualism.

King (1967) found value in black power and he spoke positively about a host of race-specific initiatives. King (1967) spoke and wrote about the merits of affirmative action, reparations, and structural economic change. "For victims of racial oppression, specific social, economic, or legislative remedies are required," King argued (Berry 1996, 143).

Not only is King misremembered as a champion for race-neutral approaches to black-white challenges, but his association with American civil religion is also misplaced. American civil religion is a mechanism for justifying white privilege and overall black disadvantage. American civil religion unifies members of the dominant racial group across a variety of social differences. King and his life's work should not be considered as part of American civil religion or a black form of American civil religion.

King's views on race are part of a separate and larger tradition that is uniquely black. Frederick Harris is among the scholars to describe this tradition. Harris (1999) examined the empowering effect of religious culture on black political mobilization. He focused on how culture matters and understands culture not as a mediating factor but an independent contribution. In an effort to broaden the resource mobilization perspective regarding social movements, Harris argued "that the indigenous culture of politicized groups facilitates the construction of meaning for action" (1999, 134). African American religion, which was created for and by African Americans, "provides sacredly ordained legitimacy to political action" (Harris 1999, 135). African American Christianity speaks "directly to the structures of oppression with causes of black suffering" (Harris 1999, 136), which American civil religion does not and cannot do because its aim is to promote and consolidate whiteness at the expense of blackness and black people.

African American religion, not American civil religion with which some scholars have tried to associate King and his thoughts on race, helps black "actors make sense of political goals by developing indigenously constructed meanings drawn from shared worldviews, languages, religion, experience, and history" (Harris 1999, 136). Whereas, in American civil religion God is present, in African American religion "God himself is politicized" (Harris 1999, 153).

King's association with colorblind ideology and reduction of his life's work to a few lines in a historic speech are just two of many issues in understanding efforts to explain ongoing racial disparities without adequately addressing race. Michael Brown and his colleagues (2003) described colorblind ideology as a way of whitewashing race. The scholars said beliefs about race rest on the following tenets: 1) The civil rights revolution was successful. 2) Racial differences persist because black people do not take advantage of opportunities. 3) The United States is becoming colorblind. Brown et al. (2003) also observed that benefits for white people were so natural that they are taken for granted. Racism is misunderstood and viewed as a remnant of the past. "A very different picture emerges when racism is understood as a sense of group position and as the organized accumulation of racial advantage, a system best understood by observing actual behavior" (Brown et al. 2003, 43). Moreover, Brown et al. contended that "much of the opposition is based on resentment toward blacks, and the resentment is driven by a fear (conscious or not) that the interests of whites as a group are jeopardized by color-conscious policies" (2003, 56).

The law supports the benefits of being white in America: "The law and large institutions normalize white advantage by articulating and enforcing cultural norms, which help to maintain racial hierarchy in the United States" (Brown et al. 2003, 56). Colorblind ideology, argued Brown et al., "has become a powerful sword and a near impenetrable shield, almost a civil religion, that actually promotes the unequal status quo" (2003, 58).

The consequences of embracing colorblind ideology as opposed to color-conscious programs and policies are far-reaching. Michael Buozis addressed some of the consequences in a 2018 article about police violence in Baltimore. Buozis said colorblindness is "crippling the ability of those in urban governments to reform police conduct and procedures, to institute civilian review boards, and to make sure police charged with brutality and homicide will see impartial judges that are not influenced by those state governments resisting the sweeping changes needed" (2018, 48).

There are a number of examples of colorblind initiatives. The introduction of Proposition 54 in California in October 2003 is just one example (Chow and Knowles 2015). Proposition 54, known as the Racial Privacy Initiative, would have prohibited state and local governments from classifying individuals by race, ethnicity, color, or national origin for the purposes of public education, public contracting, and public employment. The proposed law could be applied broadly to all state operations. The legislature could make the case that the collection of race-specific data was necessary by two-thirds of both houses. The signature of the governor would also be required. Law enforcement, court orders, and consent decrees would be exempt. According to the proposition, supporters of the Racial Privacy Initiative claimed checking a race box was demeaning, divided people, and increased attention on physical characteristics, such as skin color and national origin. Opponents of the Racial Privacy Initiative claimed that without accounting for race racial disparities would remain private. The proposition did not pass but received millions of votes in support of it.

Why White Backlash

White backlash is a dangerous thing. King (1967) wrote extensively about white backlash, far more than he wrote, or spoke, about his oft-quoted dream. King (1967) identified white backlash as the true source of black disadvantage in America. King wrote, "It would be neither true nor honest to say that the Negro status is what it is because he is innately inferior or because he is basically lazy and listless or because he has not sought to lift himself by his own bootstraps" (1967, 71). King added, "to find the origins of the Negro problem we must turn to the white man's problem" (1967, 71). King (1967) placed the responsibility of the status of black people at the feet of white people.

King (1967) understood white backlash as an expected outcome of the racialized American social structure as opposed to some occasional anomaly enacted upon black people by a few extremists. King (1967) highlighted the role of religion in the oppression of black people in America, an observation that points to the group's wholesale exclusion from American religion, which used religion to create walls of protection around whiteness and American civil religion. King (1967) argued that both religion and the Bible had been used to support the racial social order in America, and he wasn't referring simply to the days of slavery but throughout time. King (1963) was publicly critical of white clergy for their roles in maintaining the racial status quo during his lifetime. King's famous "Letter from the Birmingham Jail" was just one of many places where he offered a scathing critique of white Christians, especially white church leaders.

King authored the letter in April 1963 in response to a letter/ advertisement placed in a national newspaper by a group of Alabama clergy representing every major world denomination. In the letter the clergy described a nonviolent campaign in Birmingham as both unwise and untimely. The clergy thought more negotiations were more prudent than direct action. Peaceful demonstrations would only incite hatred and violence, the group argued. They encouraged law enforcement to keep the city safe from violence and urged black people in the city to withdraw their support. Racial change in the city should come through the courts and not by way of the streets.

King (1963) issued a response, authored primarily from solitary confinement in a Birmingham jail cell. King (1963) addressed claims that direct action was inappropriate and poorly timed (Carson 1998). He also addressed accusations that King did not belong in Birmingham because he was not from the city, a claim King dismissed on the basis of his organizational ties and his commitment to fight justice anywhere in the United States (Carson 1998). King (1963) likened himself to the Apostle Paul who went about sharing the gospel of Jesus Christ. King said he was "compelled to carry the gospel of freedom beyond" his place of birth (Carson 1998, 189).

King (1963) was dismayed by the clergy's concerns about the direct action and their lack of concern for the conditions that necessitated the demonstrations. While the clergy blamed King and others for inciting hatred and violence, King said "the city's white power structure left the Negro community with no alternative" (Carson 1998, 189). King went on to explain all of the efforts he and others took to negotiate with those in positions of power and their repeated unwillingness to operate in good faith (Carson 1998).

One of King's most important criticisms of the clergy group's concerns was regarding the timing of the demonstrations. Much like many of today's scholars, elected officials, and residents, including some black scholars and black elected officials, the clergy group did not find that direct action was politically feasible, or in King's words "well timed" (Carson 1998, 191). King's retort is much needed today. King said, "Frankly, I have yet to engage in a direct-action campaign that was 'well timed' in the view of those who have not suffered unduly from the disease of segregation" (Carson 1998, 191). What is unique about the present danger of promoting race-neutral policies and strategies in the face of the same types of social issues King sought to address in his letter and in the direct-action campaigns is that some people who have suffered from the consequences of racial injustices in America have joined the chorus of voices that sound very much like the group of eight Alabama rabbis, bishops, and reverends who wrote the original letter.

King made it plain as to why black people could not wait for a more politically feasible time. The following excerpt from his letter could be updated slightly to apply to the experiences of black people today. King was commenting on how difficult it is for black people to wait when you have seen vicious mobs lynch your mothers and fathers at will and drown your sisters and brothers at whim; when you have seen hate-filled policemen curse, kick, and even kill your black brothers and sisters; when you see the vast majority of your twenty million Negro brothers smothering in an airtight cage of poverty in the midst of an affluent society; when you suddenly find your tongue twisted and your speech stammering as you seek to explain to your six-year-old daughter why she can't go to the public amusement park that has just been advertised on television, and see tears welling up in her eyes when she is told that Funtown is closed to colored children, and see ominous clouds of inferiority beginning to form in her little mental sky, and see her beginning to distort her personality by developing an unconscious bitterness toward white people; when you have to concoct an answer for a five-year-old son who is asking: "Daddy, why do white people treat colored people so mean?"; when you take a cross-county drive and find it necessary to sleep night after night in the uncomfortable corners of your automobile because no motel will accept you; when you are humiliated day in and day out by nagging signs reading "white" and "colored"; when your first name becomes "nigger," your middle name becomes "boy" (however old you are), and your last name becomes "John," and your wife and mother are never given the respected title "Mrs."; when you are harried by day and haunted by night by the fact that you are a Negro, living constantly at tiptoe stance, never quite knowing what to expect next, and are plagued with inner fears and outer resentments; when you are forever fighting a degenerating sense of "nobodiness"—then you will understand why we find it difficult to wait. (Carson 1998, 192)

King (1963) was particularly concerned with the lack of support from the white church on the horrific experiences of black people in Birmingham and beyond. He found such white moderates, in many ways, as more dangerous than members of the White Citizen Council or the Ku Klux Klan (Carson 1998, 195). The white moderate who, including white church leaders, "paternalistically believes he can set the timetable for another man's freedom; who lives by a mythical concept of time and

who constantly advises the Negro to wait for a 'more convenient season'"
(Carson 1998, 195).

For King, time was neutral and not socially constructed (Carson
1998). White moderates mistakenly understood time "from the strangely
irrational notion that there is something in the very flow of time that
will inevitably cure all ills" (Carson 1998, 196). On the contrary, King
claimed, "we must use time creatively, in the knowledge that the time is
always ripe to do right" (Carson 1998, 196).

While King conceded that some white church leaders made sacrifices for the movement, their numbers were far fewer than he anticipated
(Carson 1998). King expressed great disappointment in the white church
and its leaders. Instead of being allies, "some have been outright opponents, refusing to understand the freedom movement and misrepresenting
its leaders; all too many others have been cautious than courageous and
have remained silent behind the anesthetizing security of stained-glass
windows" (Carson 1998, 199). While the white church and its leadership
could have used their capital to "reach the power structure," they did not
(Carson 1998, 199–200). Furthermore, King described the white church as
being complicit in the ongoing oppression of black people in the city. "Far
from being disturbed by the presence of the Church, the power structure
of the average community is consoled by the Church's silent—and often
even vocal—sanction of things as they are" (Carson 1998, 201). Such is
the case today with white moderates, and even some black scholars and
black elected officials, as they give in to white backlash and embrace
race-neutral policies and programs as the relative inferior status of black
people on a host of social and demographic outcomes remain at epidemic
levels, such as in the case of the overrepresentation of black men in fatal
police-involved shootings, black asset poverty, racial wealth inequality, and
underresourced and disinvested schools and neighborhoods.

Based on this reading of King's work, and not just a cursory analysis
of a few lines from his "I Have a Dream" speech, it is clear that King was
not only not an interpreter or champion of American civil religion, he was
one of its greatest critics. For King, American civil religion represented
one of the greatest examples of the perversion of professed American
values and ideals. This is particularly clear when King wrote, "The greatest blasphemy of the whole ugly process was that the white man ended
up making God his partner in the exploitation of the Negro" (1967, 79).
Indeed, King wrote, "White America has been backlashing on the fun-

damental God-given and human rights of the Negro for more than three hundred years" (1967, 87).

More contemporarily, philosopher George Yancy has written about his experiences with white backlash. Yancy (2018) described the reactions of white people to a letter he published in 2015 in the *New York Times.* The letter, which was published in the days leading up to the Christmas holiday, was framed as a gift, as an offering of love. Yancy's intent was to assist white America in seeing their whiteness and the ways in which they benefit from the way American society is structured, even when they think they are intentional about living in ways that are more tolerant and reflective. Yancy notes that just because there are some white people who do not use racial slurs or openly support white nationalist groups doesn't mean they are not beneficiaries of racism and complicit in a variety of ways. Although Yancy anticipated some negative reactions to his letter, he did not anticipate the hatred-filled white backlash he endured as a result of it. He was threatened with bodily harm, among other things. He had to alert campus police about threats. Yancy chose to expound about the backlash he experienced as a result of the 2015 letter and use it as an opportunity to take a deeper dig into how racism functions and the roles that individuals and institutions play. Yancy's (2018) audience for the book *Backlash* is white Americans and his truth is the oppression and suffering of black people, as the metaphysical and paradigmatic other, historically and in contemporary times.

Stephen C. Finley, Biko Gray, and I also wrote about the backlash that black professors, like George Yancy, faced in response to comments they made on social media or in their classrooms during the course of doing what they were trained and hired to do (Finley et al. 2018). Scholars like Tommy Curry, Zandria Robinson, and Keeanga-Yamahtta Taylor were targeted by virtual mobs and, in several cases, were abandoned by, or chastised by top administrators at their respective colleges and universities. Other black professors have reported white backlash for statements they have made verbally or in writing. Some of these professors canceled invited lectures and other speaking engagements for their safety and the safety of their loved ones. The threat of white backlash is real and has serious consequences. Even when black scholars, and others, take calculated measures to minimize white backlash, they remain susceptible to all types of harm. Harkening back to Yancy's love gift to white America, we find that the noted philosopher attempted to soften the blow of his hard-hitting message by using himself as a model. In his letter, and later in his book, he describes himself as sexist and discusses all the ways that he tries to be intentional about dismantling sexism but still finds himself complicit in the perpetuation of it and a beneficiary of his spoils. Yancy acknowledged that the experiences of black women, and other women of color, differ from that of white women, but avoids delving into a complicated discussion about black men, black manhood, and white hegemonic patriarchy. Nonetheless, he uses himself as a model to deflect criticisms that he is placing a lot of blame on white America but, like many black people, fails to engage in a deep process of self-reflection. While Yancy's willingness to be open about his position in society as a man provides great insight, it also takes away from the main purpose of the letter, his book, and other brilliant publications he has authored on race. Even George Yancy, as brave and as honest a scholar that he is, has experienced what he calls the vitriol of white backlash and negotiates what he says and how he says it, which can have negative implications, including undermining the very message to white America he wanted to send. In effect, Yancy does not guide white America away from white innocence but lulls them further into a sense of security in it.

We cannot let white backlash win. There remains a danger in not confronting racism in America for fear of white backlash and embracing race-neutral programs and policies. In the next few chapters we will explore the dangers of race-neutral programs and policies concerning wealth, education, and the criminal justice system.

CHAPTER TWO

Wealth, Inclusivity, and Exclusion

Racial wealth inequality and black asset poverty have persisted throughout the United States since the first group of black people involuntarily settled in Jamestown, Virginia, some four hundred years ago through the present day. Efforts to narrow the racial wealth gap and lower black asset poverty vary. Among the more recent initiatives gaining scholarly attention, and political popularity, are baby bonds (Wallace-Wells 2018). Baby bonds typically include the allocation of a specified amount of money at birth, which may not be accessed until certain conditions are met and/or may only be accessed for selected purposes, such as to pay for college tuition. Critics of baby bonds, and similar programs, point to challenges associated with implementing the initiative and securing adequate funding. Implied in the criteria for baby bonds is the fact that baby bonds will already privilege those with means and not those who have been historically marginalized economically. Which is to say, missing from the discussions of concerns about how baby bonds, and the paternalistic and universal requirements associated with them, is a conversation about how the initiative fits within broader social, political, and economic efforts that treat black bodies as problems, as pathological, while benefiting those who have been the greatest recipients of such policies, generally whites. I contend that baby bonds, like many public policies aimed at addressing racial wealth inequality and black asset poverty, do not go far enough (Martin 2019). Primarily, the baby bond programs typically do not include race-specific eligibility requirements. Moreover, baby bonds do not address the tendency of both scholars and elected officials to center whiteness (often implicitly), to use whiteness as normative and the standard by which all other groups are judged. Baby bonds also fail to anticipate and/or acknowledge repressive responses of the dominant (white) racial group to perceived black progress, in general, and to perceived black economic progress, more specifically, reactions which can best be described as religious, and when such responses are anticipated flight versus fight is increasingly becoming the preferred response. As I observed earlier in the book, I understand religion not as related only to social institutions; rather, I see religion as an orientation of understanding one's place in the world (Long 1999).

Wealth Inequality in America

Wealth inequality is a long-standing social problem in America. It is an expected outcome of any capitalist society where some *have* and some *have not*. While this is not a new phenomenon, it is one that has garnered increased attention in recent decades. Since the early 1990s, scholars have discussed ways, for example, to increase assets for the poor. The mid-1990s saw the publication of a book that pointed to wealth differences among those with similar income levels (Oliver and Shapiro 1995). The early 2000s was marked by a mass movement, which drew attention to the 99 percent without many assets, commonly referred to as Occupy Wall Street (Martin, Murphy, and Moore 2018). Perhaps the most important catalyst for discussions about wealth inequality in the past few decades came on the heels of the bursting of the housing bubble and the financial crisis referred to as the Great Recession (Martin 2013). Some banks were deemed too big to fail and were bailed out at the same time that average Americans dealt with foreclosures on their homes, one of the most pronounced symbols of the so-called American dream (Goodman 2008). The extent of wealth inequality in America has grown over time despite all of the scholarly attention and the attention the topic has received in the press and among policymakers (Kochihar and Cilluffo 2017).

Emmanuel Saez and Gabriel Zucman (2018) examined changes in the distribution of wealth in America over time in their article, "Wealth Inequality in the United States." The scholars found that since 1913, the concentration of wealth was high in the early 1900s. Wealth concentration fell somewhat between 1929 and 1978 but has continuously increased since that time. Saez and Zucman's (2018) analyses of data from the Survey of Consumer Finances, estate and income tax returns, and tax records for foundations, also revealed that the top 0.1 percent wealth share increased from 7 percent in 1978 to 22 percent in 2012. The share of wealth held by the top 0.1 percent in 2012 was comparable to the share of the top 0.1 percent in the late 1920s. The bottom 90 percent wealth share increased through the mid-1980s and then declined.

According to a recent article published in *Forbes* magazine, the richest 10 percent of Americans held 60 percent of household wealth in 1989 (da Costa 2019). By 2018, the richest 10 percent of Americans held 70 percent of household wealth. The article, written by Pedro Nicolaci da Costa, stated that the share of household wealth for the top 1 percent increased from 23 percent in 1989 to 32 percent in 2018. Da Costa (2019) also reported that the share of household wealth for households in the fiftieth and ninetieth percentiles dropped to 29 percent between 1989 and 2018. Moreover, da Costa's (2019) reporting also revealed that the bottom half of households saw virtually no net gain in wealth during the same time period. The share of household wealth for households in the bottom 50 percent decreased from 4 percent to 1 percent over the thirty-year period (da Costa 2019).

An analysis of *Forbes*'s list of the richest people in America by Inequality.org, a project of the Institute for Policy Studies, highlights changes in wealth inequality in America in recent years. For example, it is shown that Jeff Bezos (founder of Amazon), Bill Gates (founder of Microsoft), and Warren Buffett (noted investor) who topped the list of the nation's four hundred richest Americans had a combined net worth that was greater than the total wealth of the poorest half of Americans. The average net worth for someone on the list in 1982 was about $590 million in contemporary dollars. The person at the bottom of the list had a net worth of over $200 million in today's dollars. In 2018, the average net worth for a member on the list was $7.2 billion, with the lowest member on the list reporting an overall net worth of over $2 billion: "Inequality is skyrocketing even with the *Forbes* 400 list of America's richest. In today's dollars, the net worth of the richest member of the *Forbes* 400 has soared from $5 billion in 1982 to $160 billion in 2018, far outpacing the gains at either the *Forbes* entry point or average" (Inequality.org, 1). While the rich have gotten richer, the poor have not only gotten poorer, but those at the bottom have increasingly "dipped into 'negative wealth'" (Inequality.org, 1). While most of the wealth for Americans in the bottom 90 percent is in their homes, the majority of the wealth for the most affluent Americans is in such assets as stocks and mutual funds. Americans at the bottom also hold the dubious distinction of holding nearly 75 percent of the nation's debt (Inequality.org).

Racial Wealth Inequality

While the wealth gap in America is vast and showing no signs of narrowing, the disparities are even greater when race is considered. This is especially true for the black-white wealth gap. Melvin Oliver and Thomas Shapiro are among the foremost experts on racial inequality in America. Their now classic book *Black Wealth / White Wealth* reignited interest in wealth inequality in America, especially racial wealth inequality in America, among sociologists, and others. In a recent article the scholars published in the academic journal *Contexts*, they discuss ways to disrupt the racial wealth gap and begin by stating just how much of a problem differences in the types and levels of assets owned are for black households relative to white households in the United States. Put simply, Oliver and Shapiro (2019) proclaim, wealth matters and race is central.

Citing data from the most recent Survey of Consumer Finances, Oliver and Shapiro (2019) wrote that black families in the middle have about $17,000 in net wealth. Whites families have over $170,000 in net wealth at the median. Analyzing data from a sample of black and white families drawn from the Panel Study of Income Dynamics collected between 1984 and 2015, Oliver and Shapiro (2019) found that black family wealth increased from about $4,000 in the mid-1980s to $17,000 in 2015. White family wealth increased from nearly $90,000 to $275,000 during the same time period. Oliver and Shapiro (2019) also found that the average white adult who attended college had more than seven times the wealth of a black adult who attended college. On average, white single parents had more than double the wealth of the average black two-parent household (Oliver and Shapiro 2019). White households with a full-time worker had more than seven and a half times the wealth of the average black household with a full-time worker (Oliver and Shapiro 2019).

Data analyzed by Rakesh Kochihar and Anthony Cilluffo of Pew Research (2017) found that although the Great Recession of 2007–2009 harmed American household wealth across racial and income groups, black household wealth was particularly hit hard. The median net worth of white middle-income families was three times greater than that of black middle-income families in 2007, nearly four times greater in 2013, and four times greater in 2016. Pew Research identified several key trends (Kochihar and Cilluffo 2017). Black wealth for middle-income families was cut in half by the Great Recession. Taking a deeper dive in racial disparities in wealth by income, the findings also showed that white lower- and middle-income households had four times as much wealth as black families (Kochihar and Cilluffo 2017). The median wealth of middle-income black households declined 47 percent between 2007 and 2013 (Kochihar and Cilluffo 2017). The median wealth of white middle-income households declined by 31 percent during the same time frame: "From 2007 to 2013, among those in the middle-income tier, the white-to-black wealth ratio increase from three-to-one . . . these margins did not diminish from 2013 to 2016" (Kochihar and Cilluffo 2017, 5).

Causes and Consequences of Persistent Racial Wealth Inequality

The causes of wealth inequality, of racial wealth inequality specifically, are varied. As previous research has shown, explanations tend to focus on culture or structure. Culture arguments tend to focus on the need for behavior modifications for individuals and/or groups. Cedric Herring and Loren Henderson (2016) provided an overview of several other common themes that could best be understood as cultural arguments for wealth inequality. Herring and Henderson (2016) correctly noted that cultural themes often include attention to family structure, attitudes, and values. Lisa Keister (2000), in her book *Wealth Inequality in America*, focused on the role of family arrangements in explaining racial wealth inequality. William Julius Wilson (1987), author of such sociological books as *The Truly Disadvantaged*, also linked racial differences in family arrangements to variations in overall economic well-being, among other factors. Black people, arguably the most common targets of culture arguments, are said to lack self-control (Hamilton and Darity 2010). Thus, racial wealth inequality can best be understood as the result of poor savings habits among black people, for example (Herring and Henderson 2016). Black people are unwilling to delay immediate gratification and have a greater tendency to engage in conspicuous consumption than white people, adherents to the cultural argument contend (Herring and Henderson 2016).

Structural explanations point to the roles of institutions in creating and exacerbating racial wealth inequality (Evans and Wilkins 2019; Flynn et al. 2016; Leong 2013; Stanfield 2011). Jodi Melamed (2015), writing about racial capitalism, discussed what some scholars call primitive accumulation of wealth, which includes physical violence of dominant racial groups against others. War, land-takings, and colonialism are just some of the examples of primitive accumulation that were often state sponsored or state sanctioned through direct action or through intentional and benign neglect (Melamed 2015). Race and economic inequality are not merely linked, argued Melamed (2015) and others (Robinson 1983). "Procedures of racialization and capitalism are ultimately never separable from each other" (Melamed 2015, 77).

Jennifer Morgan (2015) seemingly agrees with Melamed's (2015) expression of the importance of slavery, Jim Crow, and other structures and institutions in understanding racial wealth inequality. Morgan (2015) wrote, "To engage fully and openly with the afterlife of slavery, with the problems of the past, with its silences and its reverberations in this moment in time feels not just compelling, but crucial" (155–156).

Mehrsa Baradaran recently published a book on the history and legacy of black-owned banks. Baradaran (2019) described the separate and unequal banking and credit systems in America for black and white people that kept and continue to keep black people largely asset poor. Baradaran (2019) made this clear in the statement that "the color of capital, commerce, property, trade and money was white" (5). Baradaran (2019) condemns cultural explanations regarding the black-white wealth gap, pointing instead to such problems as segregation, racism, and government credit policy as catalysts for racial wealth inequality in America historically and in contemporary times. "Instead of recognizing that white-run institutions have been complicit in and even benefited from black America's poverty, the state has repeatedly placed the burden of closing the wealth gap on the black community itself" (Baradaran 2019, 278).

Additionally, racial differences in student debt, returns on investments, and other predatory lending practices also cause differences in wealth for black and white people in America (Sullivan et al. 2015). Herring and Henderson (2016) add redlining and denied business loans to the long list. Moreover, racial differences in inheritance are also cited as a cause of racial wealth inequality, whereby white people in America are not only more likely than black people in America to receive an inheritance, but they also receive the inheritance at higher levels (Oliver and Shapiro 1995). Intergenerational transfers may be understood as reflective of perspectives that privilege culture over structure in explaining racial wealth disparities. Some might say doing so is a reflection of a certain mindset and sense of values, including feeling a sense of obligation or duty to one's offspring. Intergenerational transfers could also be viewed as structural because they represent, in many ways, the cumulative advantage of wealth inequality by race over time.

Oliver and Shapiro (2019) highlighted the importance of understanding the racial wealth gap from a structural as opposed to a cultural perspective. "Racial equity needs to be our North Star, pursued within policies regarding individual, family, or social mobility" (Oliver and Shapiro 2019, 21).

Regardless of whether the emphasis is placed on culture and behavior or on structure, the consequences of the racial wealth gap are numerous (Martin 2013). Janelle Jones, an economic policy analyst at the Economic Policy Institute, identified a number of disadvantages associated with the racial wealth gap. Black people in America are less able to transfer their income to meet future spending demands than white people in the nation (Jones 2017). Black people in America experience more asset poverty (Martin 2013). Asset poverty "measures the extent to which American households have a stock of assets which is sufficient to sustain a basic needs level of consumption during temporary hard times" (Haveman and Wolfe 2004, 145). While the racial wealth gap may have positive implications for members of the dominant racial group in America, the implications for black people in America are, to put it lightly, tragic. Racial wealth disparities keep black people in a perpetual wealth feedback loop, which places black people in the current and in future generations in virtually the same relatively disadvantaged positions as their ancestors (Traub et al. 2017). Melvin Thomas and his colleagues (2019) put it this way, "If each generation of African Americans has to start over in terms of wealth accumulation, then the relative lack of wealth for the entire population is perpetuated" (233).

Narrowing the Gap

The enormity of the racial wealth gap in America cannot be understated. By some estimates, it would take at least two centuries to narrow the racial wealth gap (Holland 2016). Over the past few decades, a number of policy proposals and programs were introduced to address wealth inequality, with specific claims or objectives of narrowing or ending the racial wealth gap. These policies and programs include Social Impact Bonds (SIB), Individual Development Accounts (IDA), Child Development Accounts

(CDA), and baby bonds. There are a number of differences in the designs, implementations, objectives, and evaluations of each, but they all have the dubious distinction of failing to address the centrality of race in wealth inequality, in general, and the centrality of race in explaining black-white wealth inequality. In short, they do not go far enough in addressing race. In general, each initiative is universal and progressive, will have limited impact on the black-white wealth gap, and does not go far enough. Evaluations of the initiatives also provide lip service to structural theories of wealth inequality, while simultaneously privileging behavioral and cultural explanations (Grinstein-Weiss et al. 2007; Stevens 2009). Baby bonds are the latest and perhaps most egregious of the offending programs and policies. Unfortunately, baby bonds also garnered a lot of media attention leading up to the 2020 presidential contest.

SOCIAL IMPACT BONDS

SIB are designed to address a particular social problem. Governments look to nongovernment institutions to address social problems, particularly after the Great Recession (Roman et al. 2015). More specifically, "SIB are a financial product used to encourage private, philanthropic and/or public investors to provide upfront capital to support project-oriented service delivery by public, private, or nonprofit actors, or a combination of these actors" (Joy and Shields 2013, 2).

Etienne Toussaint (2018) identified six key stakeholders: underserved population, government entity, impact investors, social service providers, intermediary organization, and program evaluation. The stakeholders participate in what Toussaint (2018) described as four stages. The first stage involves a feasibility study. The second stage includes reaching an agreement that is structured by lawyers and impact professionals. Toussaint (2018) said implementation is the third stage, which is followed by the final stage, or the evaluation of outcomes stage. Ideally, SIB result in low financial risk to taxpayers and benefits to the target population. Additionally, successful SIB initiatives yield double-bottom-line returns on investments and social service providers increase access to much needed resources (Toussaint 2018).

SIB have gained popularity in the United States and around the world. In 2011, President Obama introduced SIB to address recidivism, workforce training, and homelessness (Toussaint 2018). The first SIB was ONE Service at Peterborough prison in the United Kingdom from 2010 through 2014 (Shanks 2014). SIB programs are also operating in Canada, Singapore, San Francisco, Nevada, and Ohio (Shanks 2014).

Daniel Neyland offered a different view of SIB. Neyland (2018) characterized SIB as antimarket devices that conceptualize social problems into investment opportunities. Maier, Barbetta, and Godina (2018) joined Neyland (2018) in identifying a number of paradoxes inherent in the design of SIB. Neyland (2018) outlined two features of SIB that highlight how they operate as a market device and contribute to paradoxes. One feature is that SIB are expected to ensure efficiency and effectiveness. Another feature of SIB is that social problems are turned into assets (Neyland 2018). The two paradoxes involve cost-effective risk transfer and evidence-based flexibility (Maier, Barbetta, and Godina 2018). Through SIB, investors are able "to use their money to achieve both a social impact and a financial return" (Maier, Barbetta, and Godina 2018, 494). In essence, "marginalized people are converted into commodities and re-packaged as derivatives by investors plying their trade in the marketplace of inequality" (Neyland 2018, 495).

CHILD AND INDIVIDUAL DEVELOPMENT ACCOUNTS

The stated purpose of IDA is typically to change behaviors and promote savings among low-income families. Jin Huang and his colleagues described IDA as designed to increase interest in asset building to complement income (Huang et al. 2016). The underlying assumption is that low-income families have low levels of savings because they lack the requisite motivation to save. In general, IDA include the creation of an account for a qualified individual, usually between $500 and $1,000, which may be used in predetermined ways, namely, toward the purchase of a home, education, or to start a business (Grinstein-Weiss et al. 2007). IDA may include matching funds from a public and/or private source (Huang et al. 2016). Some IDA target specific populations. For example, selected IDA focus on asset building for low-income people with disabilities and are described as antipoverty policies based on the notion of asset accumulation (Soffer, McDonald, and Blanck 2010).

Like IDA, CDA seek to promote savings among the poor, but focus on minors. Other goals of CDA are to expand an individual's capabilities and to make individuals more future-oriented in attitudes and behavior (Clancy et al. 2016). Introduced in the early 1990s by Michael Sherraden, founding director of the Center for Social Development at Washington University in St. Louis, CDA are opened at the time of birth. Both IDA and CDA may only be used for approved purposes and are universal, and enrollment is virtually automatic (Clancy et al. 2016; Shanks 2014; Sherraden et al. 2018; Stevens 2009).

Saving for Education, Entrepreneurship, and Downpayment (SEED) for Oklahoma Kids, funded by Ford Foundation, and other foundations, is among the largest programs (Clancy et al. 2016). SEED is in partnership with the Corporation for Enterprise Development, the Center for Social Development at Washington University, the University of Kansas School of Social Welfare, the New American Foundation, and the Aspen Institute Initiative on Financial Security, among others, and is described as an "experiment" (Marks et al. 2014, 1). Participants were randomly assigned into groups where some participants received savings accounts and some participants did not. "The theory behind the SEED program is that long-term investment has the potential to produce a wide range of benefits" (Marks et al. 2014, 2). Designers of the largest SEED program are interested in understanding patterns of participation, measuring how much is saved, assessing the impact of matching contributions, determining barriers to saving, understanding parents' expectations and behaviors about their children's education and life opportunities, and the "cognitive, emotional, and social development . . . and . . . attitudes and behaviors concerning education" (Marks et al. 2014, 3).

Guy Feldman (2018) made the argument that it may be too soon to declare IDA successful. Claims that IDA have "the potential to reduce poverty [are] overrated and premature" (Feldman 2018, 181). IDA, for Feldman represent a retreat from public assistance to asset building and result in efforts to "re-fashion people into disciplined market actors who save and accumulate capital so as to enhance their own capacities and better compete in a market-centered society" (2018, 187).

BABY BONDS

The term BB dates back to the mid-1930s when President Franklin D. Roosevelt introduced bonds in very low denominations. Manning Marable is credited with using the term in the late 2000s to describe endowed trusts given to individuals at birth and accessible at the age of eighteen years old (Hamilton and Darity 2010). Much like CDA, IDA, and SIB, BB are designed so that they are universal, progressive, and may only be used to purchase selected assets. BBs are federally managed trusts with various monetary values. BB in the amount of $50,000–$60,000 would be available for those in the lowest wealth quartile. BB have a guaranteed 1.5–2 percent annual growth rate (Hamilton and Darity 2010).

Life bonds are similar to baby bonds (Attard 2012). According to Jamie Attard (2012), life bonds are market-traded, zero-coupon bonds that go to 10 percent of children born living below the poverty line. Only one life bond is permitted per family. Eligible participants must be born in a hospital. The bonds are vested when the child reaches the age of five and only after evidence a child is nourished and vaccinated. The bond increases in value if particular milestones are met. Life bonds are publicly traded financial securities. Death before the age of twenty-five ends all bonds. Records are maintained on an online biometric registry. Life bonds are intended to be the "voice of the poor and leveraging power of financial markets to reduce poverty" (Attard 2012, 1–2).

Elected officials have gravitated to BB. US Senator Corey Booker has introduced a plan. The plan includes a $700 billion social wealth fund over an eighteen-year period. In the nineteenth year there is an annual return on that fund plus current revenue that is consolidated to provide an annual lump sum grant to eighteen-year-olds (Bruenig 2019).

Race and Violent Financial Instruments in America

While many of the financial instruments discussed here aim to fight poverty, BB are among the instruments most closely tied with addressing the racial wealth gap and yet, like SIB, CDA, and IDA, BB are not race specific. How can a program adequately address the racial wealth gap in America and not significantly address the issue of race? There are a number of reasons for the exclusion of race from the design of BB programs. Race-specific policies are considered "political unfeasible" (Aja et al. 2014a, 42). While efforts to compensate black people for centuries of disadvantages have consistently been met with hostility, the current political climate is characterized by a heightened sense of white rage the fervor of which can best be understood as religious (Finley, Gray, and Martin 2020).

Instead of meeting the challenge of white rage head-on, some scholars and policymakers are retreating. Far too many people, some well meaning, are in essence hiding behind colorblind rhetoric rooted in neoliberal philosophies with the all too familiar refrain that race-neutral programs are race-fair programs where everyone wins. History has shown that this is rarely the case, particularly when it comes to black people. One need only look to President Ronald Reagan's trickle-down economics or affirmative action programs. Black people did not fare well under Reagan's economic programs, to say the least, and white women have been among the greatest beneficiaries of affirmative action programs. Race-neutral programs, such as BB programs, can best be understood as not going far enough to narrow the centuries-old racial wealth gap. BB programs, as they are currently constructed, represent yet another potential form of financial violence for black people in America and could be understood as another form of state-sanctioned and state-sponsored denial and/or minimization of the black suffering in America.

It might be hard for some Americans to view financial instruments as violent. However, scholars such as Zenia Kish and Justin Leroy have eloquently made this argument in the past, as shown in their effort "to historicize the violence of financialization" (2015, 630). Although Kish and Leroy showed how financial instruments, such as SIB, "transform subjects considered valueless into appropriate, even laudable, objects for financial investment" (2015, 630), I argue that the exclusion of race-specific language in BB programs specifically reaffirms that black people and their experiences in America, both historically and in contemporary times, are problematic. Black people may be used as objects for financial investment in a variety of ways but are not worthy of the humanity, dignity, and justice of compensating them for actions that made the current racial wealth gap possible.

The exclusion of race-specific language in BB programs ignores the linkages between such things as slavery, Jim Crow, and ongoing racial discrimination to the current racial wealth gap. Throughout American history black people's bodies were "made available for investment" and now BB programs refuse to acknowledge that by offering child trusts to anyone regardless of color. BB programs, by being race neutral, are "revaluing racialized life" (Kish and Leroy 2015, 631). BB programs answer the question, how do black lives matter? The answer is, emphatically, they do not; "all lives matter." Implicit in this retort is that race is not the determining factor in racial wealth inequality today. Deviant culture is to blame for black people being at the bottom of the American social structure and, therefore, no specific notice of their past and ongoing economic suffering by white people in the form of redress is required. An apology hundreds of years later is considered sufficient (Lewis 2016).

The design of BB programs "presuppose[s] that their bonded subjects enter society indebted" and the exclusion of measures targeting black people, specifically, will have the (un)intended consequences of ensuring that they remain that way for generations to come (Kish and Leroy 2015, 632). Financialization is "deeply racialized" (Kish and Leroy 2015, 632). Programs like BB are attractive to elected officials and to the general public because they appear to wed financial instruments with a commitment to equality, but the exclusion of programs specifically targeting the wealth levels of black families does quite the opposite. They perpetuate inequality and devalue the experiences of black people in America. BB programs by design represent an experiment that will again result in "new opportunities for capital accumulation for others" (Kish and Leroy 2015, 640).

It is sad that scholars who should and do know better are supporting race-neutral BB programs with claims that "the only acceptable remedial social policies are those that are facially race-neutral" (Hamilton and Darity 2010, 207). This despite earlier assertions that "the damages to the collective well-being of black people have been enormous, and correspondingly, so is the appropriate bill" (Darity and Frank 2003, 328). Such scholars engage in what they themselves have criticized others for doing, engaging in "rhetorical sleight of hand" (Aja et al. 2014a, 39), whereby the role of race is addressed as a significant determinant of racial wealth inequality and then a race-neutral solution is proposed. To add to this scholarly trickery, these scholars say, "rather than a race-neutral America, the ideal should be a race-fair America" (Hamilton and Darity 2010, 215). Failing to acknowledge and adequately compensate an entire group of people for a legacy of disadvantage, which is best measured in current racial wealth disparities, is neither fair nor just.

Jodie Melamed (2015) helps us to make sense of this racialized financialization doublespeak. Melamed said, "Yet we also increasingly recognize that contemporary racial capitalism deploys liberal and multicultural terms of inclusion to value and devalue forms of humanity differentially" (2015, 77). BB programs, I argue, are examples of what Melamed (2015) called racial cruelty, which is best described as a manifestation of what she calls the state-finance-racial violence nexus. This nexus is "the inseparable confluence of political/economic governance with racial violence, which enables ongoing accumulation through dispossession by calling forth the specter of race (as threat) to legitimate state counterviolence in the interest of financial asset owning classes that would otherwise appear to violate social rationality" (Melamed 2015, 78).

Advocates of current BB programs contend they will minimize wealth disparities between the rich and the poor regardless of race, while also acknowledging that racial wealth inequality is far worse (Boesler 2019). In fact, Zewede (2019) showed that the total racial wealth gap is over $15 trillion: "A program that annually pays out $80 million of race-neutral grants is not going to nearly close it" (2019, 8–9). Current baby bond proposals do not go far enough to narrow the racial wealth gap between black and white people in America.

Where Do We Go from Here: Fear versus Fairness

BB programs are not likely to close the racial wealth gap in America. Additionally, BB programs may also delay acknowledgments of past and present injustices suffered by black people at the hands of both private citizens and the US government. BB programs provide no race-specific redress for the injustices and offer no closure of the grievances held by black people to the injustices. There are three major objectives of reparations, a term that many scholars and policymakers, including some black scholars and black policymakers, increasingly wish to avoid addressing in meaningful ways. I agree with Toussaint (2018) in the description of the ethical challenges some have raised about the types of financial programs described here, especially as they relate to BB. Critics of programs, like SIB, say it is "wrong for someone to profit directly from the human suffering of another individual, particularly in a way that undermines the autonomy of the program participants" (Toussaint 2018, 181). For much of the history of black people in America, others have indeed profited directly from their suffering and universal programs do not adequately account for that tragic yet well-documented fact.

Conclusion: Fear or Fairness

The United States has missed a number of opportunities to right historical and contemporary wrongs where black people are concerned. The United States missed a number of opportunities to end the brutality of slavery. The nation missed opportunities throughout the Reconstruction era to secure land, wealth, and civil rights for black people. The nation missed opportunities for black people to join in the historic mass accumulation of wealth in the form of home ownership after two World Wars. America missed opportunities to capitalize on the momentum of the modern civil rights period and instead declared wars on drugs and poverty with dramatic negative effects on black communities. The nation has an opportunity with the recent scholarly and public policy interest in BB programs to address the racial wealth inequalities that have always existed but have grown to biblical proportions in recent decades by having the courage to place race not only in the program design but at the center. What path will America choose: fear or fairness?

CHAPTER THREE

From Compulsory Education to Universal Disappointment

Many Americans still view education as the great equalizer. Little has changed since the landmark *Brown v. Board of Education of Topeka, Kansas*, in that many schools are as segregated now as they were decades ago. Public schools, which should be accessible to all, are often underresourced and feeders to what scholars have called the school-to-prison pipeline (Archer 2009; "Beyond Suspensions 2019; Dancy 2014; Fasching-Varner et al. 2017; Gupta-Kagan 2019; Stanford and Muhammad 2018; White 2018). Universal pre-K programs claim to benefit black people whose children have historically had limited access to such programs, relative to white people, but racial disparities persist from the cradle through college (Gomez-Velez 2015; Morrier and Gallagher 2012). So-called school choice (Coughlan 2018; Darby and Saatcioglu 2015; Davis 2014), which on the surface appears race fair, has contributed to the continued segregation (Kozol 1991, 2005, 2008, 2019; Logan and Burkick-Will 2017) and the resegregation of public schools in America (Bell 2019; Li 2016; Wilson 2016). This is shown in the increase in gifted and talented programs within underresourced schools, and increases in charter schools (Buras 2011), magnet programs, and the like. A recent decision by a group of middle-class white residents in various unincorporated portions of the city of Baton Rouge to secede and establish their own city as a way to bypass the legislative barriers associated with establishing their own school district is another example. In this chapter I also show how the tendency to promote race-neutral educational policies in K–12 contributes to the aforementioned school-to-prison pipeline (Fasching-Varner et al. 2014; Fasching-Varner 2017) and impacts higher education (White 2018). Claims of commitments to and the value of diversity notwithstanding, education, including universal and/or race-neutral policies and programs, is not the only way, or even the best way, to a race-fair America.

History of Race and Education

For many Americans the ideas of education and democracy go hand and hand. However, long before the signatures were even dry on many of the nation's founding documents, limitations were placed upon which groups would have access to both. For much of America's early history, formal education was limited to wealthy white men. Many of the nation's early leaders were educated in one of the Ancient Eight institutions of higher education, better known as the Ivy League. As framers of a relatively new nation, these elite white men made decisions that impacted the life chances and life opportunities of those granted the benefit of citizenship and participation in the democracy and those who were regarded as property and kept out. Among the many limitations placed upon people of African ancestry during Antebellum America was the ability to learn to read and write. A number of formal and informal mechanisms were in place to discourage black people from becoming literate. Wealthy white landowners did not feel that white workers should be educated because it would interfere with their exploitation of their paid labor. Wealthy white landowners did not see any value in educating kidnapped Africans and their offspring, in large part because many believed black people lacked the intellectual capacity to learn, were subhuman, and literacy might increase the likelihood of a revolt against the oppressive system of slavery (Du Bois [1935] 1962). While some black people, both free and enslaved, did manage to learn to read and write, doing so meant overcoming a number of barriers.

For example, during the 1700s, a South Carolina law stated that any person who shall teach a slave to read or write, or cause a slave to learn to read or write, or hire any slave to do anything that involved writing, would be fined one hundred pounds (Martin 2015). More than a hundred years later, there were still many laws on the books barring slaves and other black people from learning to read and write. An 1819 Virginia code made it illegal for black people to gather in schools for the purpose of teaching reading and writing. Violators could receive up to twenty lashes (Martin 2015).

During the Civil War, the tides appeared to change somewhat with such initiatives as the Port Royal Experiment. The experiment took place in 1862 in the South Carolina Sea Islands with a goal to educate ex-slaves. The focus was on literacy, economic autonomy, and civil rights. However, the move also served as a way to assimilate newly freed men and women into the dominant society.

With the end of slavery came many challenges for black people in America, including where education was concerned. Few people have written as extensively and as eloquently about black reconstruction as W. E. B. Du Bois. Du Bois credits black people in the South as the major drivers of public education in America. Indeed, Du Bois said, "public education for all at public expense, was in the South, a Negro idea" (Du Bois [1935] 1962, 637). In *Souls of Black Folk*, Du Bois described the creation of schools for black people as one of the best things to come out of the Freedmen's Bureau, a government entity that was supposed to assist former slaves and poor whites after the Civil War. Although the original Freedmen's Bureau Act did not provide for the direct education of black people, proceeds from the rent of abandoned property were used for education, and government buildings were turned into schoolhouses. It was not until an act in 1866 that the educational powers of the bureau expanded.

Educated black people, according to Du Bois, could lead the way to greater human and civil rights for all black people. Efforts to make this idea a reality were not without risks. As Du Bois observed, "The South believed an educated Negro to be a dangerous Negro" (Du Bois 1903, 8).

Booker T. Washington, leader of the Tuskegee Institute, helped to alleviate some of the fears white people had in the South, and in areas in the North, about the risks associated with formally educating black people with the promotion of industrial education, a willingness to relinquish any title to civil rights, and an agreement that the races remain separate socially. Du Bois described Washington's industrial education program as accommodating and silent on civil and political rights (Du Bois 1903). Du Bois found Washington's call for black people to give up higher education and focus on industrial education and wealth building misguided, but it had great appeal to white Southerners and white philanthropists in the North. Instead, Du Bois (1903) said, what is needed is education according to ability. He cautioned against underestimating the ability to train black people as teachers, professionals, and leaders. Du Bois added,

"We hear daily here that an education that encourages aspiration, that sets the loftiest of ideals and seeks as an end culture and character rather than bread-winning, is the privilege of white men and the danger and delusion of black" (1903, 3).

E. Franklin Frazier, author of *Black Bourgeoisie*, addressed the influence of bourgeoisie ideals in shaping the education of black people. Great emphasis, according to Frazier (1957), was placed on professional and business education. Frazier (1957), like Du Bois before him, recalls the role of the Freedmen's Bureau in the history of race and education in America. The bureau, for example, was responsible for establishing several historically black colleges and universities (HBCUs), including Atlanta University, Fisk University, and Howard University. These institutions were to provide teacher training and higher education in the South. The establishment of schools for black people, wrote Frazier (1957), was supplemented by religious organizations, like the American Missionary Association. Frazier (1957) made the important observation that while Northern philanthropists contributed to the education of black people in the South, many were not in favor of equality. In fact, many wanted separate schools for black and white children and believed that black teachers should be paid less than white teachers (Frazier 1957; Karpinski 2006). Contrary to Du Bois's view of what should be the goal of education, Frazier concluded that Northern capitalists were not interested in "making 'men'" (Frazier 1957, 68).

Commenting on Washington's program, Frazier argued, "The schools of so-called 'industrial' education were supposed to instill in their students a spirit of humility and an acceptance of their inferior status" (1957, 69). He added, "The white workers with support of the white owning classes generally opposed the teaching of mechanical skills that would enable Negroes to compete with them" (Frazier 1957, 70). In short, schools were a "system of social control" (Frazier 1957, 71).

While recognizing the centrality of race, Du Bois ([1935] 1962) also observed there were class dimensions to education. For example, Du Bois observed that white people in the working class viewed education as a "luxury connected with wealth" ([1935] 1962, 641), whereas the black working class "connected knowledge with power; who believed that education was the stepping-stone to wealth and respect, and that wealth, without education, was crippled" ([1935] 1962, 641).

Lost in the storm of debates about trade schools and higher education is attention to the broader public school system. At the end of Reconstruction and well into the next century, public schools played important roles in maintaining the racial status quo in America. As millions of white ethnic groups from places like Southern, Central, and Eastern Europe arrived at American ports of entry, the nation contemplated how these groups would fit in with the Anglo-Saxon Protestants that were already in the country (Liberson 1980). At first, they were treated as separate racial groups. Over time, the groups were assimilated into the dominant racial group and American public schools played an important function in this process. Public schools contributed to the Americanization of white ethnic groups at the same time that they solidified the relatively low status of black people in America. While they would teach old immigrants how to be new Americans, public schools would serve as constant reminders to black people that they were worth *less* than white people and suited primarily to what white people considered menial jobs, such as domestic servants and porters.

The separate but equal doctrine established by *Plessy v. Ferguson* remained firmly intact. Black and white people in America attended separate schools that were for all intents and purposes not equal. Black teachers were paid less than white teachers. Per pupil expenditures were lower for black students than for white students. Facilities housing black students were more likely to be in disrepair than the schools housing white students. Black children often traveled far beyond their primary places of residences to attend schools that were all black because schools in the neighborhoods where they lived were exclusively for white children.

It is important to note that prior to the 1940s the levels of racial residential segregation were not as high as they are even now in many places (Massey and Denton 1993). Black and white people may have lived on separate sides of the proverbial track then but they lived in greater relative proximity to each other compared to now. For example, in Louisiana, McKinley High School was for a very long time one of the few places black people in Baton Rouge could earn a high school diploma (Martin and Jetson 2017). In the North, black students in Hillburn, New York, could not attend the Main School because it was only for white children, despite calls to desegregate all schools. It was the resistance of the black parents and the legal advocacy of then–NAACP attorney Thurgood Marshall that led to the integration of schools in the area (Martin 2015).

For many, *Brown v. Board of Education of Topeka, Kansas*, represented one of the most significant educational victories in American history. In the most general sense, the landmark case was supposed to put an end to the separate but equal doctrine in education and do so with all deliberate speed. Writing the opinion of the court, Justice Earl Warren recalled that the case centered on black people seeking admission to the public schools of their community. They were denied access to white schools because of their race. The denial was considered a violation of their Fourteenth Amendment rights. Earlier courts denied relief based upon the *Plessy v. Ferguson* ruling. The plaintiffs argued that segregated public schools were not equal and could not be equal. Warren described education then as "perhaps the most important function of state and local governments." The mere fact that public education was compulsory and the fact that so many financial resources were devoted to it highlighted the significance of education to democracy, claimed Warren. He went as far as to say that education was "the very foundation of good citizenship." He described education as a right and claimed segregation in schools "generates a feeling of inferiority." Warren addressed the negative effects of segregation on black children, while not addressing the negative effects on white children.

In the end, many hailed *Brown* as a victory for not only the modern-day civil rights movement but for the nation as a whole. Not everyone agreed that the decision was successful both then and now. The ruling was supposed to remove racial barriers in education and usher in a race-neutral era where access to public schools was race fair. Angela Onwuachi-Willig, author of "Reconceptualizing the Harms of Discrimination," highlights one of the major shortcomings of the *Brown* decision. Onwuachi-Willig noted, "Missing from the most honored race relations decision in American constitutional law is any express reckoning with racism" (2019, 354). Overlooked was the fact that "among whites during this period, it was understood that being white, regardless of how bad that white person or her life was, was simply better than being black, regardless of how good that black person or his life was" (Onwuachi-Willig 2019, 346).

Onwuachi-Willig outlined a number of the harms of discrimination that are often overlooked, including "the dehumanizing effects of believing in one's racial superiority and the damaging consequences of unchecked white privilege" (2019, 397). Such a worldview results in many members of the dominant group seeing antidiscrimination efforts as a zero-sum gain for whites. In other words, black gains mean white loses (Bell 1992a; Onwuachi-Willig 2019).

Perhaps things would be different if, according to Onwuachi-Willig, the court had not failed "to explain in *Brown* . . . that a more just world for Blacks would necessarily mean 'loses' for whites, particularly since

Brown was handed down in a society in which simply being white meant, by definition that one was better off than non-whites and better off for no reason other than whiteness" (2019, 362). In other words, the court gave the false impression "that society could achieve true racial equality without whites losing any advantages that previously flowed to them in an undeniable discriminatory society" (Onwuachi-Willig 2019, 364).

The perceived loss to white Americans resulting from the decision led to a number of creative efforts to keep the educational system in America separated on the basis of race. The efforts included the use of violence and intimidation. Protests by white parents included terrorizing black parents and black children seeking enrollment into formerly all-white schools. It also included the closure of some schools. In some cases white parents refused to send their children to schools black children attended. Still other white parents flocked to schools outside of the public school system. In many places public schools soon shifted from all-white spaces to majority black spaces. These black spaces became associated with a number of negative characteristics. Soon public schools in America were viewed as a national crisis in need of immediate attention (Duncan and Murnane 2014). The crisis was framed as one rooted in a presumed depraved black culture. Attempts at redressing centuries of racial discrimination in education were met with white backlash. The *Bakke* case was representative of the backlash.

The ruling in the *Bakke* case claimed race-conscious admissions policies violated the law and said that preferential treatment for students of color was unconstitutional (Winters 2007). In 1973 and in 1974, a white man by the name of Alan Bakke applied for admission into the medical school at the University of California at Davis. His application was rejected both times. The military veteran applied to the general admissions program. The school also had a special admissions program. In all, the school admitted one hundred students. Eighty-four of the slots were determined by a general education committee. The remaining sixteen spots were recommended by a special admissions committee. The special admissions committee was made up of mostly of nonwhite people. The general admissions committee considered applicants with grade point averages that were at least 2.5. One-sixth of the applicants were given interviews. The interviews were rated on a scale of 1 to 100. In addition to the interview summaries and grade point averages, the general admissions committee also considered each applicant's grade point average in science courses, Medical College Admission Test (MCAT) scores, letters of recommendations, extracurricular activities, and other biographical data. Prospective applicants received a benchmark score. Applicants to the special admission program did not have to meet the 2.5 grade point average requirement and were not ranked against the candidates in the general admissions process. One-fifth of special applicants were invited for interviews. Special applicants identified as either black, Chicano, Asian, or American Indian. Special admissions also received benchmark scores based upon the same materials required of applicants in the general admissions program. Over the course of four years, about sixty students were admitted under the special admissions program and forty-four minorities were admitted under the general program.

The stated purpose of the special admissions program was to address the underrepresentation of minorities in the school and the shortage of physicians of color to meet the needs of minority populations. Minority physicians were shown to better address the medical needs and concerns of minority populations than white physicians.

Bakke sued the university claiming his rights were violated when he was not admitted to the medical school. Bakke claimed he was excluded on the basis of race in violation of the equal protection clause of the Fourteenth Amendment. He also claimed the special program was basically a racial quota system. The California Supreme Court did not rule in Bakke's favor. He appealed to the Supreme Court and won on the basis that race-specific policies were not necessary to achieve the university's stated goals. The United States Supreme Court, in a 5 to 4 decision, said the special program was unconstitutional and ordered Bakke's admission into the school. In the court's opinion, Justice Powell said racial quotas were unconstitutional; race could be used to promote diversity but only alongside other factors and on a case-by-case basis. It is important to note that black, Chicano, Asian, and Native American applicants were not the only groups given special consideration in the admissions process. A 1977 article in the *Washington Post* by Lou Cannon reported that Dean George Lowery was known for favoring the children of wealthy and politically connected people with ties to the community surrounding the medical school.

Forty years after the historic decision, Mario Barnes reflected on the impact of the case on racial jurisprudence today. Barnes (2019) wrote specifically about conceptualizing programs of redress, commonly referred to as affirmative action, as a "reverse discrimination." This conceptualization of began with the *Bakke* case, asserted Barnes (2019). In the case, the court "failed to consider affirmative action as a meaningful tool for remedying racial disadvantage" (Barnes 2019, 2269). Barnes (2019) faulted the court for ignoring the centrality and structural nature of racism in America. Barnes made this clear when he wrote, "Though a court can decide it is not interested in disrupting disadvantages arising from a system of racial classification, it should still be required to acknowledge the truth of that system" (2019, 2269).

Rather than focus on the historic legacy of racism and ongoing racial discrimination, the court focused instead "on presumptive entitlements, relative merits and deserts" (Barnes 2019, 2270). Barnes's major concerns with the decision, and specifically with Justice Powell's opinion, on behalf of the court, were what he referred to as bad facts and the "conceptualization of remediable discrimination" (2019, 2273). Among the bad facts was the court's lack of attention to such things as the racial bias that contributed to gaps in MCAT scores, for example (Barnes 2019). Barnes (2019) also showed that white applicants did in fact apply to the special admissions program in 1973, although no white applicants were admitted under it.

Evidence provided by Barnes also showed that the decision not to admit Bakke was due, at least in part, to Dr. Lowery's "personal animus toward Bakke" (2019, 2275). Lowery was a dean of the medical school. Not surprisingly, Bakke did not build his case around the preferential treatment afforded the children of well-to-do people, or on Lowery's apparent dislike of Bakke, but he chose to make his stand against historically disadvantaged groups and a program aimed at righting wrongs.

Barnes said these bad facts contributed to the narrative of Bakke as a victim: "While these facts ostensibly demonstrate Bakke's denial was problematic irrespective of the existence of the Special Admissions program, the opinion treated the program as a primary barrier to his admission" (2019, 2276). Moreover, Barnes stated that the opinion of court "included a number of baffling and ahistorical determinations regarding bias" (2019, 2276).

Among the ahistorical determinations were Powell's "universalist applications of the harms of considering race" (Barnes 2019, 2277). Powell essentially characterizes Bakke as "white innocent" (Barnes 2019, 2278). Powell's focus was on "white victims'" and not on historical and contemporary racism perpetuated by the dominant racial group in America against others (Barnes 2019, 2278). He emphasized individual harm. Powell essentially asserted that *all lives matter* and that *all* groups have experienced discrimination. Powell offered what Barnes characterized as a "weak form of race-conscious review" (2019, 2283). This race-conscious review was best understood as the *diversity rationale*.

Barnes encouraged a turn away from "heavily universalist approaches to evaluating race and educational opportunity" (2019, 2284). Barnes (2019) urged American society to move away from individual blame to collective responsibility. Acknowledging obstacles, Barnes pleads, "However uncomfortable race-conscious approaches are in terms of forcing people to realize that race still matters and often carries heavy consequences, it is certainly more aligned with the world 'that is' than the world that people hope 'will come to be'" (2019, 2297). The *Bakke* case provides the backdrop for understanding not only racial jurisprudence but also race and education going forward.

This was evidenced in the publication of *A Nation at Risk*. The report, like the *Brown* and *Bakke* decisions, did not address structural racism. In the early 1980s the National Commission on Excellence in Education was formed. The report the commission created addressed the quality of education in America, which was considered in a state of crisis and thus a threat to the ideal American dream (Putnam 2015). The purpose was to define the problems and provide solutions. Like the *Brown* decision, the aim of the report was "not [to] search for scapegoats" (Putnam 2015, 2). In other words, the report did not deal with the race-specific or race-conscious efforts to limit black people in particular from receiving a quality education. Instead, the commissioners claimed to assess the quality of teaching and learning at public and private schools, colleges, and universities. The report was to focus on how the United States' educational system compared with other nations. Commissioners were also tasked with evaluating the relationship between college admissions requirements and student achievement in high school and relay best practices. Much of the focus was, however, on teen youths. The report drew from several main sources: papers, feedback from interest-holders, public meetings, panel discussions, and symposiums. Over a period of eighteen months, the commission examined educational excellence on individual, school or college, and societal levels. The commission concluded there was a need to reform the system and create a learning society. The report called for a replacement of what was referred to as a cafeteria-style curriculum. The report also included a need for better teacher preparation and an end to a shortage of teachers. There was a need, according to the report, to attract the best people to the profession. Including comparisons of outcomes from the mid- to late 1960s to outcomes of the mid-1970s through the early 1980s, the report ushered in an era of market-driven solutions to education reform.

The market-driven solutions to education reform have caused a great deal of harm to many, but especially to black students, particularly in underresourced schools. Among other things, the market-driven solutions involved new ways of assessing teachers and students and the introduction of the standards movement. The passage of the No Child Left Behind (NCLB) Act and what I call the Wal-Martization of American public schools played important roles in promoting market-based approaches to public education.

NCLB was enacted during President George W. Bush's administration. The act was based upon a program that was first implemented in Texas in 1984, called the Texas Educational Miracle (Levine and Levine 2012). The Texas Educational Miracle was developed based upon concerns that students in the state lagged behind others in the nation and were ill-prepared for the high-tech era (Levine and Levine 2012). H. Ross Perot led the Texas Select Committee on Public Education to address the challenges facing the state. Perot "emphasized tough management methods to achieve measurable results and accountability from educators" (Levine and Levine 2012, 106–107). The business model approach to public education would come to influence education in Texas and throughout the nation.

While public education is considered a political issue that is associated with the Democratic Party, it was somewhat surprising to see a great deal of political will and capital devoted to public education by a Republican administration. Nevertheless, after one of the most contested presidential elections in the nation's history, in 2000, President George W. Bush introduced NCLB. It represented a shift in the role of the federal government in public education. For much of the history of public education in America, control over curriculum, funding, and resources was at the state and local levels. After the mid-1960s, the federal government became increasingly involved in education, which raised important questions about funding, quality, separation of church and state, standards, and assessments (Martin 2015). Schools provided opportunities not only to communicate knowledge but also to share the nation's cherished values and even its important myths. Public schools serve as an important purveyor of the American civil religion (Bellah 1967).

NCLB was described by critics, including parents, teachers, administrators, and unions, as an unfunded mandate. Under NCLB, students in third through eighth grades had to be tested every year in reading, math, and science. The act outlined sanctions for failing schools (Labaree 2010). Schools identified as failing had a relatively short period of time to make changes or avoid a state takeover. Schools in need of improvement had to meet established standards by 2014. Schools were in need of improvement if they did not meet the standards after the second year. If schools were still failing in the third year, students would have the option to transfer or receive a variety of supplemental services, such as tutoring. If the appropriate corrections were not made by the fourth year, the school district would have to make corrective action. By year five, still-failing schools would have to be restructured. For example, the school might become a charter school, or replace the staff, or turn over operations to the state or to a private company (Martin 2015).

Some researchers have found that NCLB did not fulfill the manifest function of the legislation—to address the challenges facing American public schools—but did manage to make a lot of wealthy people even wealthier. Levine and Levine argued, "Charter schools have become big business" (2012, 109). Companies receive a fee for providing school management services. These companies may provide loans for startup and capital. Management companies may also lease property to charters and provide equipment, furniture, furnishings, and sell books and educational programs (Levine and Levine 2012). It is not unusual for management companies to have multiple contracts at the same time (Levine and Levine 2012). Levine and Levine (2012) also outlined the many ways people, including billionaire Rupert Murdoch, benefited from the focus on high-stakes testing and data collection and analysis. Additionally, Levine and Levine (2012) addressed the many ways that the superrich, like Bill and Melinda Gates, and others, use their resources to inform education policy (Au and Ferrare 2015).

We should think about NCLB not only as a profit machine for the wealthy but also as another form of violence enacted upon black people by the dominant racial group. NCLB is just one example of the ways members of the dominant racial group create systems and structures that harm subordinate racial groups and then blame the subordinate groups for their relatively lower status. Then, members of the dominant group create and support policies that claim to address the crisis they created. At the same time, the dominant group heaps blame upon the minority groups, which perpetuates and exacerbates the misery already heaped upon subordinate groups. The dominant group benefits in material and nonmaterial ways from the misery experienced by nonwhite groups. Sometimes the benefits are monetary, as Levine and Levine (2012) mentioned, and other times the added value is whiteness.

Connie Wun provided a very compelling argument in her article, "The Anti-Black Order of No Child Left Behind." Wun (2014) drew upon a question W. E. B. Du Bois asked many years ago: How does it feel to be a problem? (1903). Wun (2014) correctly stated that the basis for the passage of NCLB was the view that black children were a problem. In the white imagination, failing schools were made up primarily of black children, many of whom were not successful academically (Fordham 1988), due in large part to the belief that most lacked the discipline (Ferguson 2001; Morris 2016), desire, motivation, intelligence (Winfield 2007), and home training to succeed in school and in life (Delpit 2006). Black boys and girls were trapped in a school-to-prison pipeline because they violated more school policies, despite research showing that this is not the case ("Beyond Suspensions" 2019), and were destined to drop out as opposed to persisting through to graduation (Fine 1991). Hence, there were "underlying racial suppositions of the seemingly benevolent policy" (Wun 2014, 463). Using critical race theory (Dixon and Rousseau 2006; Leonardo 2013) and Lacanian psychoanalysis, Wun understood NCLB as a "symbolic order structured in anti-Black fantasies" (2014, 463), which is to say that social policy includes narratives about disenfranchisement and inequality to promote education reform that do not challenge racism. Racial disparities are identified but not much is done in an intentional and meaningful way to narrow or erase the disparities. Part of the role of the state, according to Wun (2014), is in shaping racial identities through policy. It can be shown, then, that there is a "constitutive relationship between racial fantasies, state policies, and racial formations" (Wun 2014, 463).

For Wun "the symbolic is the organizing system by which we come to see, understand, and represent reality" (2014, 465). Drawing on the works of black intellectual thinkers, such as Frantz Fanon and Hortense Spillers, Wun added, "An anti-Black conscious is central to White society" (2014, 468). Hence, "imagining Black figures as intrusive, dangerous, parasitic and different is part and parcel of the fantasy for a complete White society" (468). Wun (2014) argued that NCLB fixates on black bodies as problems. Specifically, Wun contended, "NCLB has popularized and institutionalized national attention on Black youth as problems to be solved" and is "undergirded by an anti-Black fetishization—one that renders Black bodies as perennially deficient" (2014, 469). Wun went on to write, "NCLB may be a colorblind policy reifying whiteness, but it is undergirded by a particular form of racism, anti-Black racism which positions Black in the collective unconscious as the permanent Other, regardless of whether they demonstrate otherwise . . . NCLB is a means by which anti-Blackness is written into law" (2014, 472).

While interest and investment into NCLB was halted on September 11, 2001, by the attacks on the nation, the legacy is clear, as evidenced by the many varieties of school choice programs that have increased over the past few decades, including gifted and talented programs (Barlow and Dunbar 2010; Kaufman 2013), magnet schools and programs (Martin 2015), charters schools (Frankenberg, Siegel-Hawley, and Wang 2010; Hankins 2007; Jacobs 2013; Levy 2010), and even the creation of new cities, such as in the case in East Baton Rouge Parish in Louisiana and the new city of St. George.

The bottom line is that, among other consequences, NCLB provided a way for many white parents to avoid what they had feared most and resisted for years, sending their children to school with black children. Many regretted paying taxes for schools that their children did not attend because they opted out of the public school system when integration and busing was forced upon them. Many white parents found themselves paying for expensive private schools and property taxes that helped fund public schools. In the tradition of taxpayer citizenship, white parents saw black parents and their children as free riders, as individuals upon whom education was wasted because they were culturally deficient, including lacking motivation, a strong work ethic, sound values, and the appropriate role models to be successful. Any barriers black people faced to achieving the American dream were self-imposed. Exposing white children to this inherently pathological culture would do irreversible harm in the collective white imagination and thus disrupt what Wun called "the fantasy for a complete White society" (2014, 468).

NCLB was not the last education policy to impact public schools in America. The Obama administration introduced "Race to the Top" as part of the recovery package aimed at addressing the economic crisis that became known as the Great Recession. States competed for grants based upon innovative approaches to addressing challenges in public education, especially in urban areas, which have for a long time been code for black.

As in the case of NCLB, "Race to the Top" was also undergirded by antiblack sentiments, despite being introduced by the nation's first black president. The Obama administration's educational policy was among other things generative. William Howell wrote about many of the public policies that can be connected to "Race to the Top." It could be argued that many of these policies are also rooted in antiblack sentiments with an emphasis on black students and black parents as problems, particularly in places with relatively high populations of school-aged black children.

School districts across the country have made a number of compromises to try to lure white parents and their students back to public schools (Martin 2015). It is not a coincidence that within schools that are predominately black that there are gifted and talented and magnet programs that are predominately white and/or Asian. Scholars, including Eduardo Bonilla-Silva, have written about the "honorary white" status afforded to some Asian subgroups in America. Moreover, themed magnet schools are disproportionately white. These magnet schools often focus on lucrative and emerging fields related to science, technology, engineering, and math (STEM).

For those mostly white families that cannot or do not wish to move to areas where the houses and the schools are considered "good," and that have had limited or no success gaining access to the coveted but finite spots in gifted and talented or magnet programs and schools, there are other options. In a number of cases, mostly white families have joined together and established their own cities as a way to create their own schools. One of the most recent cases, as mentioned earlier, involves efforts to create the city of St. George in Baton Rouge, Louisiana.

Baton Rouge and the Formation of the City of St. George

First, here is a bit of history about Baton Rouge. Baton Rouge was not only the historic site of plantations where hundreds of thousands were enslaved, and it was not just the site of battles during the Civil War. Baton Rouge has a long history of racial conflicts that have been met with various forms of resistance and various forms of violence. For example, in 1953, black residents in Baton Rouge started one of the first bus boycotts in the nation. In the early 1950s, a law was passed banning black-owned buses followed by increases in the city bus fare, which benefited from a largely black ridership. Fed up with standing in the back of half-empty buses, after paying their bus fare, the black community pledged not to ride the buses until things changed. Within a relatively short period of time, the black community received a number of concessions and the boycott ended. The car sharing part of the little known but historic boycott was used as a model for the better known 1955 Montgomery Bus Boycott. The Toni Morrison Bench by the Road project memorialized the contributions of the boycotters in 2016 (Martin and Jetson 2017).

Public transportation was not the only racial battlefield in Baton Rouge. Black and white people have battled over police shootings, such as in the case of the killing of Alton Sterling in 2016. Sterling was selling compact discs in front of a convenient store in north Baton Rouge when officers responded to a call. It did not take long before Sterling was on the ground and taking his last breath after being fired upon by one of the two responding officers. The killing of Alton Sterling was recorded and shared on social media. Protesters from Baton Rouge and beyond called for justice on behalf of Sterling and his family. Soon after the killing, several law enforcement officials were targeted by a man who traveled to the city from Dallas. Many were injured and several were killed. That summer, Baton Rouge also experienced a 100-year flood. The summer of 2016 revealed the continued racial divide in the city. Blue ribbons, the passage of so-called Blue Lives Laws, and other overt support for law enforcement contrasted with calls for social justice for black residents, particularly against the backdrop of what some have collectively called the Black Lives Matter movement. Baton Rouge became the symbol of the racial canyon that exists between black and white people in America. The city has been featured by the BBC and on *Frontline*, among other national and international outlets.

It is not surprising then that Baton Rouge is home to one of the longest running desegregation cases or the home of a move for white residents to secede from the city. In a report written by LSU law professor and president and CEO of Build Baton Rouge Christopher Tyson, titled "How Did We Get Here: A Brief History of Black Baton Rouge," wrote that race and education are related. Almost immediately following *Brown*, enrollment in private schools in Baton Rouge increased.

Tyson (2016) described *Davis et al. v. East Baton Rouge Parish School Board* where in 1956 black parents sued to desegregate schools and the board responded by institutionalizing "a 'freedom of choice' approach to integrating schools," which stood until Judge Parker "decided that the school board had been running a dual-school system in violation of *Brown*" (Tyson 2016, 6). Parker ordered a desegregation plan that led to the closure of more than a dozen schools and adopted "forced busing in order to achieve racial balances similar to the district's demographics" (Tyson 2016, 6).

During the first year alone, Tyson (2016) found that seven thousand white students left the school system. Tyson chronicled the domino effect of white flight from the public school system: "White residents not only left the school system, they departed entire neighborhoods—many of which were also integrating as factors such as the 1970s oil boom, the end of legal segregation, and the emergence of affirmative action in employment expanded opportunities . . . spaces legally reserved for whites only" (2016, 7).

The white abandonment of public schools and the city more broadly had lasting effects. For decades after the court-ordered busing, "whites went from a majority of public school students to a small and rapidly diminishing minority. . . . Few white families chose to remain. Property values in these neighborhoods stagnated or fell as the disproportionate wealth and wealth-creating capacity of the city's white community fled neighborhoods now stigmatized as black and thereby devalued economically and socially" (Tyson 2016, 7). Furthermore, "the school desegregation battle and its impact on the racial composition of neighborhoods led to a spatial remaking of the city" (Tyson 2016, 7).

A consent decree was reached and approved by the courts in 1996, which brought an end to busing. Busing was an approach to integrating schools that was used in many cities but failed (Delmont 2016). By that time the school system was predominately black and economically disadvantaged students: "Given the city and nation's history of racial discrimination in employment and economic opportunity, the implications of geographically concentrated, inter-generational racialized property were brought into focus through the desegregation backlash" (Tyson 2016, 7). Tyson concluded:

> The historical and structural resource disadvantages of black communities manifested themselves in both the reality and perception of student performance in schools. The city's increasingly majority black schools produced poor results, which only accelerated white and middle-class flight from the school system. The result is what many describe as a tale of two cities: a North Baton Rouge . . . and a South Baton Rouge. . . . The former is predominantly black and poor. The latter has some racial diversity and is largely upwardly mobile in character. The former has been dubbed the worst place to live in Louisiana, the latter the best. (Tyson 2016, 7)

It is in the latter place that white residents have decided to take their latest stand and secede from the city of Baton Rouge. Efforts to create a school district for the mostly white residents of South Baton Rouge were not successful and proponents were advised that establishing a city was a far more expedient route to establishing a school system. It is important to note that there is a portion of the unincorporated municipalities that would make up the city of St. George where there is a relatively high concentration of black, Latino, and relatively poor residents. The mapmakers for the city of St. George literally drew a line around this area to exclude the majority minority residents. Initially, efforts to get the required signatures to place the proposal on the ballot failed. Undeterred, proponents of the city of St. George eventually got the required signatures and also managed to limit the number of people who could vote on the proposal. While the proposal for the incorporation of the city of St. George would impact the entire city of Baton Rouge and the surrounding region, as shown in Tyson's (2016) report, only registered voters living in the boundaries of the proposed city could vote. Some forty thousand registered voters would decide the fate of the city of St. George and potentially the city of Baton Rouge and surrounding area. On October 12, 2019, residents in the target area voted and many did so in a way unseen throughout the nation, particularly in black communities. In the years leading up to the October election, polling locations in the future city of St. George were moved from the predominately poor and black sections closer to the location of housing subdivisions that would be included in the planned city. Voters were literally seen walking with their dogs to the polling place, in some cases, less than a quarter mile, to vote, while efforts to stop black people from picking up voters on Sundays, for Souls to the Polls, have been unsuccessful.

More than half of the residents casting ballots on October 12, 2019, voted to incorporate (Rojas 2019). Many of those voting in favor of the measure will tell you that it is not about race. For many black residents and for the white residents who get it, like in the case of the Powell opinion, many find such dismissals of race and racism as both baffling and ahistorical. Race mattered then as it does now (Capper 2015).

Conclusion

Clearly, the history of race and education in America informs race and education in contemporary times (Lewis 2009). Nevertheless, there is a push to "fix" problems with the educational system by ignoring or downplaying the roles of race and racism. Calls for race-fair and race-neutral policies originate from many places and not only include some of the very policies discussed earlier but also calls for universal pre-K and free college tuition for all. Much has been written about how race matters and how it impacts black people, in particular, from the cradle to the grave, and still, public policymakers and some scholars tout the merits of providing access to pre-K for all students. This allows some elected officials, in particular, to say they are doing something about an issue impacting black people but not risk falling out of the good graces of potential white voters and donors. Similarly, despite mountains of evidence of racial inequalities throughout the educational system, there are few race-conscious policies in existence or in the pipeline calling for free access to higher education for black people. In very few cases, such as in the case of Georgetown University, where research has shown the university directly benefited from the sale of a group of kidnapped Africans and now their descendants may attend without final cost to them, little has been done to redress the harm done to black people as a result of their exclusion from educational opportunities throughout the nation's history. Instead of focusing on policies and programs that redress past discrimination, discrimination that systematically kept black people out of the most prestigious educational institutions (Bradley 2018; Synnot 2010) and out of many that cannot be called by name, predominately white institutions focus instead on the rhetoric of diversity and the fortification of walls of whiteness (Brunsma, Brown, Placier 2013; Carr 2016; Hauper 2009; hooks 1988; Jones 2014; Kayoko 2016; Thein 2004; Vaught 2011; Wallerstein 2008). At the same time, the number of black students and professors is on the decline and both are endangered and vulnerable (Martin et al. 2019). It is important to tackle the tough challenge of addressing tensions between race-neutral and race-conscious approaches to public education in America (Pinder 2013; Pollock 2014; Rahl 2016; Rooks 2006; Winters 2007; Yalof Garfield 2014). Again, it is simply not acceptable to say that now is not the time to redress demonstrated acts of discrimination aimed at black people in America. It is always the right time to do what is right.

CHAPTER FOUR

The Color of Justice

Racial disparities in the criminal justice system are apparent from decisions about policing strategies to arrests to prosecutions. Nevertheless, programs and policies aimed at addressing violent crimes, curbing gang activities, and addressing quality of life issues are framed in such a way as to convince the public that they are race neutral and intended for the common good. Agents of the criminal justice system are also often viewed as race neutral and thus virtually immune from criminal prosecution in cases, for example, involving the use of excessive force against a black civilian by a white police officer. Current policing strategies and criminal justice reforms aimed at addressing ongoing injustices do not go far enough to address racial disparities and are unlikely to lead to a race-fair America.

The numbers are by now all too familiar and indisputable. Black people, especially black men, are disadvantaged when it comes to the criminal justice system when compared with other groups, especially white people, and this finding is pervasive throughout the criminal justice system. Scholars have found racial disparities at virtually every stage of the criminal justice system. A March 2018 report produced by the Sentencing Project highlighted some of the racial disparities in the American criminal justice system. The project issued the report to the United Nations on the subject of contemporary forms of racism and racial discrimination. The report stated that black people make up 27 percent of all the people arrested in the United States, which is double their share in the US population. Black youth are 15 percent of USE children but represent 35 percent of juvenile arrests. In the year 2016, black people were 3.5 times more likely to be jailed than white people. Imprisonment rates for black adults were 5.9 times the rate for white adults. Elizabeth Hinton and her colleagues at Vera Institute of Justice showed that one in three black men born in 2001 could expect to be incarcerated in his lifetime compared to one in seventeen white men. David Arnold and his colleagues showed that in the case of bail, black defendants were 3.6 percentage points more likely to be assigned monetary bail than white defendants, and black defendants receive higher bail amounts (Arnold, Dobbie, and Yang 2017). Roland Fryer's (2016) work on police use of force found that black and Hispanic people were more likely to experience some form of force in their interactions with police. Kendra Scott and her coauthors studied police shootings over a twenty-year period and found that while black people made up about 15 percent of the US population, they accounted for 40 percent of people shot and killed by police. Black suspects were five times more likely to be shot by police than white suspects (Scott et al. 2017).

Black bodies and black communities are more likely to be under surveillance than members of the dominant racial group, such that black people, whether walking, driving, or simply *being*, are more likely to have contact with the police than white people. Black people are more likely to face arrests, be detained longer, assessed higher bails, given longer sentences, and evaluated unfavorably in matters related to parole than members of the dominant group. Blackness, in the eyes of many in the criminal justice system, and in the minds of many members of the dominant racial group in America, is unredeemable. They possess an unforgiveable blackness that is manifested in black juvenile offenders placed in boot camps and wilderness programs, while white juvenile offenders are placed in rehabilitative settings, such as mental health and substance abuse facilities (Fader, Kurlchek, and Morgan 2014).

For much of American history, race and crime linked. It is important to understand the history of race and crime in America to grasp more fully why racial disparities in the criminal justice system persist and how seemingly race-neutral policies, even so-called criminal justice reform efforts, do not go far enough. Simply monitoring policies for potentially racial disparate impacts is not sufficient. Coming to terms with the role that race has played historically and in contemporary times in the criminal justice system is imperative and cannot wait for a more mythical politically feasible time.

History of Race and Crime

The law has been used as a tool to both define and control black people in America since before the founding of the nation. This sentiment is aptly captured in the title of former New York State justice Bruce M. Wright's widely read book *Black Robes White Justice* (1993). Laws were passed determining the status of black children as either enslaved or free—based upon the condition of the mother. Laws were passed placing limits on the abilities of free and enslaved black people to learn to read or write. Teaching a black person to read or to write, or to employ a black person in an occupation requiring reading and writing, was punishable by a fine or imprisonment in various states. One of the first documented uses of the law to treat black and white people differently occurred in the 1640s. Historian Darlene Clark Hine and her colleagues documented the plight of John Punch, a black indentured servant. Punch escaped from his employ along with two white indentured servants. Accounts bear witness to the harsh treatment that indentured servants faced during the seventeenth century. Indentured servants were contractually bound to perform labor for a specified amount of time. At the end of the contract, it was not uncommon for indentured servants to receive land. Leaving before the end of a contract could result in the extension of the contract as well as physical punishment. Punch and the others were eventually found. Each was punished, but Punch's sentence was particularly harsh. Punch was sentenced to servitude for life. Throughout the enslavement era, black people—both free and in bondage—were subject to legal and extralegal efforts to control every aspect of their lives for the benefit of the dominant racial group. This was especially clear from the establishment of slave patrols to the deputizing of everyday white Americans as part of various fugitive slave acts to apprehend black people seeking freedom. It was viewed as the duty of white people to maintain the physical bondage of black people and they were financially rewarded for doing so. In his famous speech on the meaning of the Fourth of July to the American Negro, Frederick Douglass pointed to the ridiculous number of laws pertaining explicitly to black people and the contradictions and hypocrisy associated with regarding black people as less than human while at the same time expecting black people to follow the law.

Efforts to control the black population through the use of the law did not end with the reunification of the nation after the Civil War. In many regards the reach of law extended further than in previous times, in part because many members of the dominant racial group in America felt it had to be far reaching to maintain the racial hierarchy that characterized the nation. During this time, while black people were seeking to secure land, a quality education, and reunite with family members, former veterans of the Confederacy were establishing social clubs that functioned to terrorize black people. The lynching of black people increased exponentially during Reconstruction, and thereafter, with law enforcement officials joining lynch mobs or refusing to hold participants responsible for their actions. Thousands of black people across the country, particularly in the South, were lynched allegedly for assaulting white people, trying to vote, owning land, or simply because they were black. Despite antilynching campaigns, the practice of killing black people and law enforcement officials from the police to judges looking the other way continued for many decades. Some scholars have argued that recent lethal police-involved shootings of mostly black men represent just one of many contemporary forms of lynching. At the same time that trees were bearing strange fruit, the nation was capitalizing on a system that functioned a lot like slavery. Convict leasing benefited from the passage and enforcement of vagrancy laws, for example, and other tactics to further criminalize black people. Convict leasing depended upon the arrest, sentencing, and incarceration of black bodies that were later contracted out to private companies, among other entities, often for the benefit of local sheriffs and the surrounding communities. The practice lasted for decades and negatively impacted the lives of those directly affected, as well as their families and their communities of origin. Anthony Braga and his colleagues described convict leasing as part of "the intentional association of blacks with dangerousness (i.e., criminality)" (2019, 542).

Sadly, American history is filled with examples of racial disparities in the criminal justice system. Some of the more notable examples include the destruction of Black Wall Street in the early 1920s, the multiple convictions of the Scottsboro defendants, and the murder of fourteen-year-old Emmett Till. The Greenwood district in Tulsa, Oklahoma, was once home to one of the most prosperous black communities in the nation, which made the black residents targets of the ire of their less affluent white neighbors. The trigger that ignited what became known as the Tulsa Race Riots of 1921 was an incident involving a black elevator operator, Dick Rowland. He was accused of sexually assaulting a white women in a department store elevator. Rowland was arrested and a white mob later arrived at the place where he was detained. The mob was committed to enacting their form on justice. A group of black residents, including some who were armed, also gathered at the site where Rowland was detained in an effort to protect him and due process. Someone fired a shot and a riot broke out. During the riot the wealthy black neighborhood was burned to the ground. Law enforcement officials rounded up black residents, allegedly for their own protection, leaving their community without protection. Black armed residents could not physically protect their homes, business, and communities, and evidence from a commissioned report later showed that some law enforcement officials participated in the assault on Greenwood, while others merely looked away. To add insult to injury, an ordinance was passed making it too prohibitive for the black residents to rebuild. The history of Black Wall Street, while known to historical figures like Booker T. Washington and others, remained relatively unknown well into the later part of the twentieth century.

More than a decade after the destruction in Tulsa, another American tragedy took place in the early 1930s highlighting the ways in which the law was turned against black people in a show of force that clearly supported dominant narratives about black people and crime. In the early 1930s, many people in America were living in relatively poor conditions. Poor economic outlooks in places like the Deep South drove poor white men and women, as well as poor black men and women, out of their hometowns to larger cities where they hoped the economic outlook was better. Such was the case for a group of black boys and men, most of whom did not know each other prior to the day that would forever change their lives, and eventually, change American jurisprudence. Nine black boys and men, Clarence Norris, Andrew (Andy) Wright, Leroy (Roy) Wright, Haywood Patterson, Charlie Weems, Ozie Powell, Willie Roberson, Eugene Williams, and Olen Montgomery, hopped on a train in Alabama headed for Tennessee. On the same train were two poor white women, Ruby Bates and Victoria Price. The white women were discovered on the train at a stop in Scottsboro, Alabama. Rather than face time in jail for riding the rails without a ticket, the women accused the nine black males of raping them on the moving train. The nine black males were immediately arrested and were soon sentenced to death. A conviction of the crime of rape carried a mandatory sentence of anywhere from ten years in prison to a death sentence. The mere accusation by two white women that nine black men assaulted them was more than enough evidence for the arresting officers, prosecutor, and judge to convict them on multiple occasions. Were it not for the intervention of the Community Party of America and their desire to exploit the case to advance their views about capitalism, the Scottsboro defendants, as they came to be known, would have died at the hands of the state, instead of tragically dying of a host of unnatural and natural causes later in their lives. It would be more than half a century before all of the Scottsboro defendants were pardoned and the State of Alabama admitted that the nine black boys and men accused of violating Bates and Price never did anything to them. The case, although not as well known as it should be, led to two important Supreme Court decisions, which makes the point that others have made—that black people are often teaching members of the dominant group about their history, Constitution, and forcing them to come to terms with gaps between who and what they say they care about and value as opposed to how they actually function in society and in the world.

Indeed, at the time of the trial, the defendants found it almost impossible to find someone to represent them. The families of the defendants were able to pay a real estate attorney to represent them initially. The poor representation and the overturning of their original death sentence led to the historic *Powell v. State of Alabama* case. The case was argued on October 10, 1932, and decided on November 7, 1932. The Supreme Court ruled that it was the right of every defendant in a capital case to have the aid of counsel based upon the due process clause of the Fourteenth Amendment. The defendants, who were tried in three groups, did not meet with counsel "until the very morning of the trial, no lawyer had been named or definitively assigned to represent the defendants," according to Justice Sutherland, author of the opinion on behalf of the court. Sutherland warned in the opinion that a defendant "must not be stripped of his right to have sufficient time to advise with counsel to prepare his defense. To do that is not to proceed promptly in the calm spirit of regulated justice, but to go forward with the haste of the mob."

The second historic case associated with the Scottsboro tragedy, *Norris v. Alabama*, was argued on February 15, 1935, and decided on April 1, 1935. It involved the exclusion of black people from a grand jury. The Supreme Court found that the State of Alabama had indeed denied the defendants their right to equal protection under the law by the systematic exclusion of black people from juries. The list of prospective jurors examined by the court included the names of only six black people. The names appeared in a different color ink at the bottom of an alphabetized list containing only the names of white county residents. It was clear to the court that the names had been hastily added and were not part of the original document. The court also considered testimony from longtime residents that no black person in anyone's recent memory had ever served on a jury, although there was evidence that no less than two hundred black residents were qualified to serve on juries. Justice Hughes wrote the opinion for the court and highlighted testimony from the Commission of Jurors to underscore antiblack sentiments that kept black people from participating on juries. Hughes recalled testimony by the commissioner in which it was stated that there were no black people in the county who were honest and intelligent enough to serve. The commissioner also stated that he was unaware of any black people in the county who were of good character or sound judgment. The commissioner added that he was unaware of any black people that were not alcoholics or plagued with disease that were physically capable of serving. The commissioner found all black people in the county to be unfit, illiterate, and possessing a history of crimes involving moral turpitude. Hughes countered the commissioner's comments and stated, "We find it impossible to accept such a sweeping characterization of the lack of qualified negroes in Morgan County."

Few lessons were learned from the Scottsboro ordeal, which lasted for many years. This was evident in the case involving the killing of Emmett Louis Till. Emmett Till was a fourteen-year-old black boy from Chicago, Illinois. His mother, Mamie Till Mosley, allowed him to travel to Mississippi in the summer of 1955 with relatives. Till entered a store with his cousins to purchase candy. It was alleged that Till whistled at a white woman, Carolyn Bryant, while in the store. Frightened, Till and his companions left the store and returned to Till's great-uncle Moses Wright's home. Sometime after the incident, two armed white men awakened Till and his family in the middle of the night and left the house, bringing Till with them. The men were Roy Bryant, the husband of Carolyn Bryant, and his brother, J. W. Milam. Wright later testified that he thought the pair might punish Till and then return him to the home. Neither Wright nor his other family members considered that Bryant and Milam would torture Till, tie a seventy-five-pound cotton gin around his neck, and throw his body away in the Tallahatchie River where it was recovered days later. Bryant and Milam were soon identified as the men who kidnapped Emmett Till and both faced trials for Till's murder and for his kidnapping. It is telling that the white community supported Bryant and Milam from their arrests through their inevitable acquittals. Money jars, for example, appeared in local stores to collect money for Bryant's and Milam's defense fund. Unfounded allegations against Mamie Till Mosley and other members of her family were made. Just as in the case of the Scottsboro defendants, no black people served on either of the juries during the trials for the murder of Emmett Till and later for his kidnapping. The all-white male jury quickly found Bryant and Milam not guilty and at least one jury member remarked that they would not have taken as long as they did if they had not taken a break to enjoy a soda. It was a forgone conclusion for both sides that Bryant and Milam would not have to pay for such a horrific assault on a young black boy and the entire black community. Years later, Bryant and Milam admitted their guilt in an interview they gave to the popular *Look* magazine. Despite ongoing efforts, no one has been made to take responsibility for what happened to Emmett Louis Till, and his mother spent much of her remaining days seeking justice on his behalf. It is also noteworthy that a memorial to Till has more than once been the target of gunfire. Till's memorial is also a popular gathering place for some self-proclaimed white nationalists. Recently, a bullet-ridden memorial to Till had to be replaced. The new memorial was intentionally created out of bulletproof material. It is sad, to say the least, that such a sacred place marking a horrific event remains a racial battleground and symbol of whiteness and white supremacy.

The 1950s and 1960s were filled with efforts on the part of black people to use the justice system to ensure that they could actually enjoy the rights afforded to them under the Thirteenth, Fourteenth, and Fifteenth Amendments. Hence, the modern civil rights movement is also thought of as a Second Reconstruction. Law enforcement officials were unleashed upon black men, women, and children engaged in a variety of acts of civil disobedience and against those engaged in what were considered as more radical forms of resistance. The amount of black bloodshed, oftentimes at the hands of law enforcement officials, was incalculable and led to the passage of the Civil Rights Act of 1964, Voting Rights Act of 1965, and the Fair Housing Act of 1968. The Civil Rights Act of 1964 was supposed to remove race as a barrier to access to areas of public accommodations. The Voting Rights Act of 1965 was to eliminate obstacles to voting, including poll taxes and literacy tests, among others. The Fair Housing Act of 1968 banned racial discrimination in the rental or sale of housing. Despite the fact that each was considered a legal victory and evidence of the success of the modern civil rights movement, racial discrimination continued.

The decade ended with a number of historic revolts that were not only connected to the assassination of Dr. Martin Luther King Jr. but often involved responses to events connected with the excessive use of force by white police officers against black people. What was considered an epidemic in many major American cities prompted a call to action and resulted in the creation of a special commission, which produced the historic Kerner report. In 1968, the report described the existence of two societies in America divided by race. The report optimistically stated that racial divisions between black and white people in America could be reversed. While the report acknowledged the role of white institutions in creating, maintaining, and condoning the segregation and poverty that characterized many of the communities where the uprising took place, the report also characterized the uprising, referred to in the report as riots, as black people attacking "symbols of American society." The authors of the report claimed there were 164 disorders in 1967 between January and September, which varied in intensity. The report makes note of the partial role that police practices played in the riots/uprisings, but also cited high unemployment, inadequate housing, poor education, lack of recreational facilities, disenfranchisement in the political system, discrimination in the justice system, poor delivery of municipal services, and inadequate welfare programs. The report correctly stated that "white racism is essentially responsible for the explosive mixture which has been accumulating in our cities since the end of World War II" (Kerner Commission Report 1968, 9).

Included in the Kerner report (1968) were a number of race-specific recommendations for moving the country forward. Several of the recommendations specifically addressed race and policing. It was recommended that the police review operations and eliminate abrasive practices and offer more police protection for residents living in distressed communities. It was also recommended that there be fair redress of grievances against the police and that efforts to recruit more black officers should proceed in earnest. The authors of the report called for "a policy, which combines ghetto enrichment with programs designed to encourage integration of substantial numbers of negroes into the society outside the ghetto (Kerner Commission Report 1968, 19).

Calls to address historical and contemporary racial issues with race-conscious solutions were not heeded; rather, what followed was a white backlash that regarded race-conscious initiatives as largely antiwhite. The white backlash and responses to urban unrest were also met with what scholars have described as the Southern Strategy and the use of coded language best represented in the phrase *law and order*. Sociologist Joe Feagin, in a number of recent posts to social media, has responded to the use of the term *Southern Strategy*, and highlighted the importance of clarifying the phrase by adding the word white, thus it was, and some have argued still is, a white Southern Strategy. The strategy was created by white politicians in the South as a way to win elections by seeking to capitalize on the fears and antiblack sentiments of white voters, regardless of their political affiliation. Michael Tonry wrote about the causes of racial disparities in the criminal justice system and addressed the significant role of the white Southern Strategy. In the short term, white elected officials won elections and "in the long-term, however, it helped shape and reinforce prevailing negative white attitudes towards black people" (Tonry 2010, 280). The white Southern Strategy, according to Tonry (2010), facilitated the replacement of ideas about black inferiority with racial resentment. In other words, Tonry was arguing that there was a shift in the prevailing white narrative to include claims "that disadvantaged black people have received too much support from the state and are responsible for their own adverse social and economic conditions of their lives" (2010, 280).

Kevin Drakulich and his colleagues also published an article about the Southern Strategy some seven years after Michael Tonry. Drakulich et al. (2017) identified the 1964 election as the first stage of the white Southern Strategy. "Republicans attempted to peel large numbers of southern white voters away from the Democratic Party by appealing to their discomfort with the racial changes posed by the civil rights movement" (Drakulich et al. 2017, 9). Drakulich et al. also asserted that "racially-coded 'tough on crime' rhetoric that initially sought to criminalize those involved in political protest . . . later evolved into support for 'wars' on crime and drugs in the 1980s and 1990s" (2017, 9). The authors described the uptick in police practices and policies as part of the backlash against the civil rights movement. The upticks resulted in the mass incarceration of black people from the 1970s onward. The civil rights movement and other forms of protest against a host of injustices perpetrated on black people throughout the nation's history and in more contemporary times undoubtedly contributed to the militarization of policing in American. It also exposed heightened inequality in the justice system and ongoing antiblack sentiments manifested in the everyday actions with ordinary citizens with membership in the document group and in the daily operations of social institutions. Efforts by subsequent administrations to prove that they were hard on crime, such as in the case of the Clinton administration, also contributed to the epidemic of mass incarceration. Actions during the Obama administration, despite the establishment of a task force to address policing in the twenty-first century, also did little to address racial disparities in the criminal justice system.

Which forms of the policing of black bodies and black communities were performed varied and were *informed* by social researchers, such as in the case of broken windows policing. Robert Lombardo and Todd Lough (2007) describe broken windows as rooted in social disorganization theory, which argues that there is a direct relationship between distressed communities and crime. These distressed communities are almost always majority black communities. The idea is that there is a decline in the impact of social norms on individuals (Lombardo and Lough 2007). The decrease in the influence of existing rules of behavior leads to high rates of deviance and increased complexities of urban life. Broken windows theory understands disorder and crime as linked in a developmental sequence (Lombardo and Lough 2007). Broken windows policing strategies, according to Lombardo and Lough (2007), were based upon a foot patrol experiment in Newark, New Jersey. The popularity of such strategies is significant given the finding that "although foot patrol did not have a direct impact on crime, citizens felt safer and developed a more favorable opinion of police" (Lombardo and Lough 2007, 123). Clearly, the word *citizens* and the characterization of their opinions about the police apply more to white people than to the largely black residents subjected to the hypersurveillance of their bodies and their communities.

Jonathan Oberman and Kendea Johnson conducted research on the application of broken windows theory in New York City and linked it directly to racism. Oberman and Johnson (2016) highlighted the disparity in the Bloomberg administration's use of stop, question, and frisk. Individuals who were stopped, questioned, and frisked under the broken windows approach to policing were overwhelmingly black and Latino residents of the city. Emily Kaufman (2016) has also written about the use of stop, question, and frisk, which is part of a broader hot-spots police program (e.g., Operation Impact).

Kaufman's (2016) research described how the police department in New York City flooded high-crime areas with high concentrations of new police officers. Majority black communities, for example, became "sites of mobility constrained and structured by biometric and spatial technologies borrowed from the military" (Kaufman 2016, 72). Kaufman also found that "the profiling is racial, social, biometric, bio-political, and spatial, and works to demarcate dangerous people and places" (2016, 72). Kaufman (2016) described these tactics as bio-spatial profiling. The term refers to "an analytic that emphasizes the biometric, biopolitical, and spatial tactics by which individuals are profiled, as well as the spatial effects of such targeting" (Kaufman 2016, 74). Black residents in these communities under siege are at risk simply by "moving through, staying still, or simply *being* in public space as a person of color" (Kaufman 2016, 74).

William Bratton was a strong supporter of stop, question, and frisk. While the current major, Bill de Blasio, claimed to be against stop, question, and frisk, he too is a supporter of broken windows approaches to policing black communities and other communities of color. In the city of New York alone, there are more than forty agencies authorized to issue summons as part of these strategies, which, Oberman and Johnson said, "further denigrates and increases the marginalization of communities of color" (2016, 1079). These agencies including the New York City Police Department (NYPD), Metropolitan Transportation Authority (MTA), New York Fire Department (NYFD), American Society for the Prevention of Cruelty to Animals, Taxi and Limousine Commission, Off-Track Betting Corporation (OTB), Tax Enforcement, and the Unified Court System.

The consequences associated with being on probation or parole are many. In the case of housing in New York City, an individual must wait one to four years after completing a sentence, probation, or parole, or paying fines before they are eligible for Section 8 or New York City public housing. Oberman and Johnson (2016) also noted some of the criminal justice reforms passed as part of the de Blasio administration, which included a push for universal pre-K, greater attention to mental health, diversion to medical services as an alternative to incarceration, and reform of the bail system. However, Oberman and Johnson concluded that the reform efforts would result in a "small dent," at best, and leave racial disparities unaltered (2016, 1087). Furthermore, Oberman and Johnson wrote of broken windows policing, because it "depletes resources, destroys futures, and ruins lives of New Yorkers, there will be no reforming that can obliterate the dividing line" (2016, 1089–1090).

Some critics of broken windows theory support the community impact hypothesis. This hypothesis is more focused on how informal social control can be implemented It is also referred to as community-building, or the "process by which the police strengthen the capacity and resolve of citizens to resist crime by building positive relationships with community residents (Lombardo and Lough 2007, 128). The community impact hypothesis is described by Lombardo and Lough as "intelligence-led policing" (2007, 133).

Gary Stewart (1998) offered yet another perspective on the problems associated with broken windows theory and broken windows policing in his work on civil injunctions and gang activity. Stewart described "modern anti-gang civil injunctions as a legacy of postbellum vagrancy ordinances" (1998, 2250). Civil injunctions are characterized by the authorization of broad police and judicial discretion to control "undesirable but innocent minority groups" (Stewart 1998, 2250). To the point of the present book, Stewart asserted that use of "purportedly race-neutral anti-gang civil injunctions threatens to harm minority communities" (1998, 2250). One of the key limitations of broken windows theory and broken windows policing is the "blindness to the potentially harmful impact of broad police discretion on minority communities" (Stewart 1998, 2254). Black and brown people are regarded and treated as public nuisances without the benefit of the constitutional rights afforded to others. "Civil injunctions were designed to circumvent the rule of law" (Stewart 1998, 2278).

Researcher Tanya Erzen also offered a perspective on the limitations of broken windows theory and broken windows policing. Erzen (2001) argued that broken windows theorists use the term *community* often but seldom define it. Erzen asked, "Who is the community being protected? Who or what is disorderly? Does cracking down on quality-of-life offenses reduce crime? And, most importantly, does the Quality of Life initiative result in more daily police violence and harassment?" (2001, 20–21). These, and other critical questions, are seldom asked or answered in the literature on broken windows theory, nor are they addressed in the actual practice of broken windows policing.

Victor Rios (2006) offered yet another critique of broken windows theory and broken windows policing in his article on the hypercriminalization of black and Latino male youth and mass incarceration. Rios (2006) showed how broken windows sees black people and many other people of color as broken people. Broken windows policing involves the treatment of all black youth, for example, "as criminal suspects" (Rios 2006, 50). Rios added, "Poor racialized bodies are managed as criminal risks" (2006, 52).

Brenden Beck, in a 2019 article on broken windows and race, found that broken windows theory and broken windows poling was not merely an urban phenomenon. Beck (2019) showed that much of the research on broken windows was conducted within an urban context. Beck (2019) wanted to determine how police responded to demographic shifts in the suburbs with quality of life arrests and how those responses compared with activities in American cities. Beck (2019) cited the killings of Michael Brown in the suburban town of Ferguson, Missouri, and the killing of Philando Castile in a suburban town in Minnesota as examples of recent high-profile cases where black men were stopped for relatively minor matters that quickly escalated resulting in their deaths at the hands of white officers.

Beck (2019) explored the application of broken windows theory relative to several others, including racial threat, benign neglect hypothesis, and place theory. Racial threat holds that the larger the nonwhite population, the more the dominant white group will rely on social control strategies to maintain their position, such as in the case of policing. Benign neglect holds that as more poor and nonwhite people move into an area, white people respond with abandonment and may simply move away. Race and place theory states that as nonwhite and poor populations increase, police actually decrease arrests. The latter theory anticipates racial impacts, such as racial profiling. Beck concluded based upon his research that "demographic and economic shifts are changing quality-of-life policing in the typical suburbs" (2019, 287).

Recommendations for effective policing strategies and for criminal justice reform are varied and may avoid race-conscious language altogether, or include proxies such as poverty and class, or broad terms, such as culture or community. For example, the National Institute of Justice (NIJ) (2017), described as "a leader in developing and advancing the research agenda for policing" (v), outlined a strategic research plan for 2017–2022. The agenda included a number of priorities including the promotion of research on police training and education. More specifically, the aim would be to "examine and assess the impact of police training on cultural competencies" (NIJ 2017, 3).

Another objective of NIJ's strategic research plan is to study and evaluate police decision-making. Support would be made available for research that examines "the impact of organizational and cultural change within agencies on police-citizen encounters involving police decision-making" (NIJ 2017, 6).

Strategic priority number three in the NIJ (2017) plan is to promote and support research on the relationship between policing and communities. The most historic and ongoing racial tensions involving police and the larger criminal justice system are between predominately white police forces and black communities. The unwillingness of the NIJ and others to make this plain is a large part of the problem in the failure to address historic and ongoing racial disparities in the justice system. Talking around the issue of race will not move the country through, or past, the issue of race; rather, ignoring, minimizing, and merely hoping it will go away only exacerbates the problem. And yet, the objectives listed under the aforementioned strategic priority are racially generic. One objective includes evaluating community engagement strategies. Another objective attempts to address the issue of building trust and confidence between police and communities. A third objective will promote research on the role of individual and community characteristics on policing services. More specifically, this third objective would address the *fear of crime* and community perceptions. There is no mention of examining the impact of the *fear of police* many black communities experience. An appreciation of, and acknowledgment of, the significance of race would yield important objectives that were missing from the current strategic research plan.

The state of Louisiana is at the bottom of most lists ranking states on such matters as quality of education and positive health outcomes. However, Louisiana has long topped the list of states with the highest rates of incarceration in the nation. In fact, for many years, Louisiana has been a world leader in the number of its citizens it sends to jails and prisons. Recently, bipartisan efforts to remove this shameful moniker from the state of Louisiana were passed and hailed as a model for other states. A report published in 2018 by the PEW Charitable Trusts outlined Louisiana's criminal justice reforms. The report cited many of the reasons Louisiana was the state with the highest incarceration rate for many years. The causes included the high numbers of nonviolent offenders, longer prison terms, and narrow guidelines surrounding supervised parole, criminal justice–related debts, and a lack of support for victims ("Louisiana's 2017 Reform" 2018). The reform package would prioritize inmates based upon the degree to which the inmate posed a threat to the public. Criminal justice reforms in Louisiana would also strengthen community supervision, eliminate barriers to reentry, reinvest money saved from reforms to reduce recidivism, and provide greater support for victims. When we take a deeper dig, it is clear that it is not only too early to celebrate but that perhaps no celebration is in order.

According to an article written by Noah Lanard, "Louisiana Decided to Curb Mass Incarceration, Then ICE Showed Up," and published in *Mother Jones*, Louisiana passed a reform bill in 2017, which resulted in fewer people going to jail and the release of inmates more quickly. However, the spaces freed up by these inmates were soon filled when Immigration and Customs Enforcement (ICE) began housing immigrants they detained. ICE housed immigrants at three new jails in Louisiana, which doubled the agency's capacity by February 2019. ICE contracted with local jails in locations with relatively few immigration lawyers. An overwhelming majority of the asylum claims made by the detainees were denied. The three jails run by LaSalle corrections, a Louisiana-based private jail operator, adopted a successful model used in the nursing home industry, which involved keeping occupancy high and costs low. ICE pays the private jail operators more for the detainees than the state paid per inmate. Louisiana pays $24 a day to imprison individuals and ICE pays more than $60 per detainee. In Bossier Parish alone, more than 180 inmates were moved to make room for ICE detainees. Located in the town of Plain Dealing, about a thousand immigrants are currently detained. The local sheriff, Julian Whittington, reportedly commented that the new arrangement was not only better for the local area economically but added that the immigrants are better behaved. Whittington's comments imply antiblack sentiment and reflect an unfortunate overgeneralization about black inmates and by extension black people.

Tonry (2010) offered some radical recommendations for addressing racial disparities in the criminal justice system, which include both race-neutral and race-conscious language. Tonry called for "radical decarceration; fundamental changes in drug policy; repeal of mandatory minimums, three-strikes, and life-without-possibility-of-parole laws, and creation of new mechanisms for reducing the sentences of historically unprecedented length" (2010, 307). A "less radical" approach would include assisting practitioners in becoming more aware of racial stereotypes and colorism, which might be achieved through such things as racial disparity audits to assess disparity impact projections. What Tonry (2010) considered "less radical" is perhaps most radical in the current political climate in America. While Tonry (2010) goes further than most in bringing race to the center of conversations about criminal justice reform, simply monitoring a problem is not the same as fixing it.

Braga et al. (2019) recommend that police not rely heavily on surveillance and enforcement actions to address poor relationships between the police and black communities. Recognizing that it "greatly matters how the police approach crime problems in places" (Braga, Brunson, and Drakulich 2019, 537), Braga et al. argued, "community policing should be the foundation of any police-led violence reduction strategy" (2019, 547). For this to be possible some immediate reforms include reductions in investigatory stops and the use of body cameras. Braga et al. clearly understand that "the racially problematic history and contemporary practices of American policing suggest that issues may be rooted in more than mere ignorance" and "required a direct challenge to [racial] hierarchy and the structures that preserve it" (2019, 549). Finally, Braga et al. make the following sobering statement about poor and/or black communities that are simultaneously over- and under-policed, "The central tragedy is that these communities that are subject to the most aggressive and harmful police strategies, and who have the least confidence in the police, are also the most dependent on their services" (2019, 549).

Race-neutral attempts to address persistent racial disparities in the criminal justice system are harmful. Hinton et al. (2018) contended that race-neutral laws perpetuate racial inequalities. These laws include drug-free zone laws, habitual offender laws, hot spot policing, zero tolerance, prosecutor bias, racial differences in bail practices, and pretrial detention. Hetey and Eberhardt (2018) presented several important strategies for addressing the use of myths to justify persistent racial disparities in the criminal justice system, which would focus more attention on race and racism. One potential strategy is to offer context. Framing the inequality should enhance understanding about contemporary racial disparities. Hetey and Eberhardt (2018) also think that challenging the association between black people and crime is critical. White people who associate black people with crime must be forced to confront their beliefs and become more educated on the subject of race. A third potential strategy offered by Hetey and Eberhardt (2018) is to highlight the role of institutions. So much of the focus on racial disparities in the criminal justice system is on the behaviors of individuals. More attention to the roles of institutions and the impact of institutions, through such mechanisms as changing public policies, might address misconceptions about the linkages between race and crime.

Ngozi Kamalu and colleagues made a similar set of recommendations that not only included alternatives to desperate sentencing and incarceration practices but also suggested that judges, attorneys, and other law enforcement officials take a history class and receive effective training to enhance their understanding about race and racial disparities in the criminal justice system and their role in it.

Perhaps Judge Bruce Wright understood best the continued significance of race and the danger in denying the impact of racism on the American justice system. He wrote, "Thoughts about the judicial system and the racism of America that [spill] over into that aspect of existence that purports to epitomize impartiality, objectivity, and fairness" (Wright 1993, 50). While some have recommended increasing the number of black police officers, black prosecutors, and black judges, Wright (1993) warns that skin color cannot be the only eligibility criteria. Wright described some black judges, along with some other black people, "who claim respectability and allow that mirage to keep them quiet and from being actors in the necessary drama needed to change an oppressive society" (1993, 51). He described these black people as particularly dangerous to social justice causes because they essentially serve as "instruments of continued oppression" (Wright 1993, 51). This group of what Wright calls Afro-Saxons "believe that bitterness is a lack of . . . gratitude that blacks should feel for America's blessings" (1993, 52). In other words, they are uncritical of the systems that perpetuate racial disparities because they see themselves as merited beneficiaries or as evidence of black exceptionalism. It is important to note that the answer to addressing racial disparities in the criminal justice system is not simply to have more black police officers, black prosecutors, or black justices, but to fundamentally transform the racialized social structure of the criminal justice system, to have more people inside and outside of the system working to make it more equitable and be real about race.

Gary Younge echoed the judge's sentiments in comments made on the unrelated subject of the role of journalists in questioning information regarding the Brexit deal from unnamed sources. His comments apply to the need for black people in the academy, in the criminal justice system, in elected positions, and beyond to not voluntarily participate in their own oppression and the oppression of others. Younge (2019) wrote, "In a period of rampant inequality, entrenched division and diminishing trust, we are most effective when we challenge the powerful, not when we embed ourselves among them."

The problem is not as it has historically been framed. It is not a black problem, argued Wright (1993). It "is really a white one, deeply rooted in traditional racism" (Wright 1993, 57). And the burden has been and continues to be on black people to educate the nation on its own history and value claims, which for some, contributes to what some scholars call racial battle fatigue and other forms of stress. "Blacks have by their lawsuits run a coast-to-coast classroom in which they have sought to teach whites the true and humanitarian meaning of their own invention of democracy" (Wright 1993, 61). The unwillingness of many white people to learn from these valuable lessons has contributed to the religious fervor on full display today. Instead of the cases showing the great distance between racial groups, "many whites began to believe that blacks were getting ahead" (Wright, 1993, 62). This belief has caused some members of the dominant racial group in America to respond in often threatening and violent ways both in the virtual world and in the real world. It is for that reason that some scholars, elected officials, journalists, and everyday citizens, including many identifying as black, fear addressing race as a way to address inequalities in the criminal justice system. Based upon the current political climate, it does not appear that it is feasible to address such matters, which begs the often asked questions, If not now, when?

CHAPTER FIVE

Resistance and Racial Progress

Kaepernick and the Practice of Leadership

Black athletes were some of the most successful figures in nineteenth-century America, including Abe Hawkins. Hawkins was an enslaved jockey on Ashland Plantation in Ascension Parish, Louisiana. Little is known about Hawkins's efforts to fight back against the horrific institution of slavery. His desire to be free is, however, clear. Hawkins left Ashland Plantation as soon as the federal troops arrived and enjoyed a successful career as a free jockey in New York. Contemporary athletes are often compared to enslaved athletes like Hawkins. Given that black athletes today do not live in physical bondage, the expectations are that they will act in the interest of the entire black community and not only in their own self-interests. The degree to which black athletes identify with the larger struggle for racial justice has been an ongoing debate. However, Colin Kaepernick's recent protests to bring attention to a host of racial injustices is clear and convincing evidence of a renewed interest in using one's social position to draw attention to issues that matter to some but should matter to most. While a great deal of attention has been devoted to discussions about Kaepernick's chosen method of protest, little to no attention is devoted to how Kaepernick's protest contributes to broader ongoing debates and controversies regarding racial progress, racial uplift, and leadership in the

---

Portions of chapter 5 were previously published in L. L. Martin, "The Politics of Sports and Protest: Colin Kaepernick and the Practice of Leadership," *American Studies Journal* 64 (2018), Web, 19 May 2018, DOI 10.18422/64-06.

black community, especially as it relates to centering race in discussions about persistent racial disparities.

In this chapter, I argue that Kaepernick's protest is part of a larger discussion involving black intellectuals about whether racial progress is possible and how best to achieve it. I draw from the works of Booker T. Washington, W. E. B. Du Bois, Evelyn Brooks Higginbotham, Derrick Bell, and Frank Wilderson III, as each presents unique sets of ways of measuring racial progress, in general, and black progress in particular. A race-fair America should be characterized by measurable evidence of racial progress. I show that despite Kaepernick's concerns that his actions might not actually lead to changes in the hearts and minds of people, or in social institutions, he nonetheless sought to demonstrate his power, his agency, and in doing so, showed other black athletes that there was victory in the fight, a need to call out race-based injustices, and that leadership was not about a position one occupied. Kaepernick showed—in the tradition of adaptive leadership—that leadership is a practice and he mobilized black athletes and others to respond to one of the nation's most enduring activists challenges—racial inequality. In the past, black athletes like Michael Jordan and Tiger Woods were criticized for not saying more about race (Martin 2017). More recently, black athletes like Kaepernick are taking on the issue of race directly (Martin 2018), even as some other so-called black leaders have gone silent.

Racial Uplift and a Policy of Submission

In the decades before the Civil War, black people and white people debated about what would happen were slavery to end. Both black and white people, not all, supported emigration to places outside of the United States, such as in the Caribbean, and countries in Africa. Other black and white people believed that black people could eventually enjoy their rights as free persons, as total human beings, and equal partners within the nation's boundaries but disagreed on how long such a feat would take, and how best to achieve it.

In 1895, Booker T. Washington was invited to address a group gathered at an exposition in Atlanta, Georgia, to highlight just how much progress both the region and black people made toward recovering from the material, social, cultural, economic, and political effects of slavery and the aftermath of the Civil War. Washington's remarks paint an interesting picture about the experiences of black people during slavery and how black people ought to prepare themselves for the future that lies ahead. His remarks also pointed to the important roles white people in the South and in the North would play to facilitate racial progress and black uplift.

Washington addressed the largely white audience at the 100-day event, Cotton States Exposition. One of the days was devoted to showcasing the work of black people in areas such as agriculture, including Washington's students at the Tuskegee Institute. Washington told the audience that success will depend on how whites in the region and outside of the region deal with their persistent problem or burden—black people.

Washington described himself as a spokesperson or leader for the majority of black people. In doing so, he thanked the organizers for allowing black people to participate in the event for a number of reasons, including the fact that black participation was tantamount to recognition of the value and manhood of black people. Washington also asserted that the gesture would lead to cementing a friendship between black and white people going forward. Perhaps Washington sought to exploit the idea of white virtuosity, that whiteness is always true, pure, and good, and therefore, no matter the atrocities and violence associated with the enslavement system and the period thereafter, black people always remained or desired to remain friendly and loyal to white people.

While Washington viewed black people as important to the overall economic development of the South, he made certain to address any concerns white people might have about collaborating with black people. Washington assured the group that working with black people to achieve economic progress in the South would not cut into white privilege or upset their preferred hierarchical racial social system by describing black people as ignorant and lacking in experience.

According to Washington, the period following the Civil War represents a new life for black people, signifying an alleged end to a social death, which R. L. defines in "Wanderings of the Slave" as slavery. Booker T. Washington went on to say that it was unthinkable that black people would seek political positions and not focus on the acquisition of land or an industrial skill, as both were mutually exclusive. Washington viewed owning a dairy farm or a truck garden as far more important than occupying a position in a statehouse.

Washington not only advised black people to not set their horizons on political power, but he also urged black and white people to look toward each other and not to other groups and places as they sought to achieve greater economic progress in the region and in the country. The South, argued Washington, was where black people would enjoy their greatest success. For it was one of the few places where black people would be "given a man's chance." It was in the South, according to Washington, that people would succeed "by the productions of our hands." Moreover, Washington stated, "it is at the bottom of life we must begin, and not at the top." Washington clearly cosigned on the existence of, and rationalization for, a racialized caste system in the region and in the nation. He told white people that he agreed with the inferior status of black people and the established racial hierarchy. He also communicated to black people where he thought they rightfully belonged as they made "the great leap from slavery to freedom."

Slaves were extremely loyal, friendly, dedicated, loving, forgiving, and not resentful toward slave owners and this undying devotion that has been thrust upon enslaved athletes like Abe Hawkins would carry into the nineteenth century, according to Washington. Booker T. Washington cited many examples of the loyalty of slaves toward white people, especially white people directly involved in the daily oppression of the enslaved. Slaves, said Washington, were willing to give their own lives in defense of white lives, and would continue to do so into the foreseeable future. The same could not be said for the immigrant groups reaching America's shores at the time of his address. Black people needed help and encouragement from white people. Not only did Washington encourage a paternalistic relationship between white people and black people where white people would continue to dictate all areas of black life and get credit for their benevolent gestures, but white people would also benefit economically. Washington assured the white audience that they would continue to profit off the actual and the surplus labor of black bodies as was the case during the enslavement era and throughout the post-enslavement era in America.

Black progress would not come quickly, warned Washington. Not only would black progress require help and encouragement from white people, it would also require their financial resources. Washington was the beneficiary of white philanthropy and thanked funders for their socially responsible investments into combating the so-called Negro problem. He also assured the predominately white audience that the idea of social equality was a nonissue for him and for most black people, particularly because he and other black people realized that they were ill-prepared to carry out the rights and responsibilities bestowed upon them by God and by the law.

Washington's view about what was required for racial progress and the impact of slavery on that outlook was not as widely accepted as indicated in his remarks in Atlanta. John Hope, one of the founders of the Niagara movement, expressed his disagreement with Washington's sentiments in his remarks on February 22, 1896, in Washington, DC, before a debate society. Hope was clearly not in favor of abandoning calls for social inequality; rather, he said black people should "demand" social equality. Hope did not think black people should accept a position at the bottom of society. He did not think they should be satisfied or content there. He urged black people, instead, to "be discontented. Be dissatisfied." Unlike Washington's accommodating and conciliatory tone, Hope said, "We shall not have to plead for justice nor on bended knee crave mercy; for we shall be men. Then and not until then will liberty in its highest sense be the boast of our Republic."

During the year John Hope made his comments to the debate society, the US Supreme Court ruled in the *Plessy v. Ferguson* case, which challenged segregation on public transportation and ushered in the doctrine of separate but equal, which Washington endorsed in his Atlanta Compromise speech. Writing the dissenting opinion, Judge John Marshall Harlan said white people think they are the dominant race, a position Washington agreed with and acknowledged in his 1895 address. Harlan said that white people "will continue to be for all time" and that the arbitrary separation of the races, which was cemented by the court ruling, shall serve as a "badge of servitude" and a "thin disguise of 'equal accommodations.'" Washington, in his address a year earlier, was telling black people to put on a badge of servitude and he provided assurance to white people that black people would wear it with pride. Harlan's comments on the court case also point to the fact what Washington hoped to achieve was a thin disguise of racial progress.

Du Bois and Social Justice

W. E. B. Du Bois authored a critique of Washington's address in one of his published books in 1903. Du Bois used the terms adjustment and submission to describe how black people like Abe Hawkins were forced to respond in relationship to white people. He characterized Washington's speech as fitting nicely into this old way of engaging with the oppressor. While Du Bois viewed Washington's approach as antiquated, he also viewed it as particularly dangerous given a number of other important factors. Du Bois cited the rise of globalization, increased racial tensions, and a great focus on economic development in the South that made Washington's appeal to white supremacy, white virtuosity, and white privilege so potentially damaging to black people, to racial progress, to democracy.

Du Bois criticized Washington for accepting the belief that black people were inherently inferior. He described Washington's approach as very submissive. While Washington evoked the idea of manhood several times in his address, especially black manhood, Du Bois calls those proclamations into question. Manhood, for Du Bois, was not just about land and houses. Du Bois equated manhood with exercising the right to vote.

The idea that improving the quality of life for black people in the United States might require some form of industrial training and progress or land acquisition is not an idea with which Du Bois disagreed. What Du Bois did appear to take issue with was Washington's dismissal of the need for political rights and political power, without which none of Washington's goals could be achieved. Industrial progress simply could not happen so long as black people could not vote, did not have civil equality, and black youth were not educated in the liberal arts and other fields.

It was not racial reconciliation to which Du Bois objected; rather, he objected to Washington asking black people to engage in demeaning themselves. Du Bois opposed racial reconciliation: Supporting Washington's brand of racial reconciliation, claimed Du Bois, would be disastrous.

Despite disagreements with Washington's main arguments about the status of black people and the best way to promote economic progress in the South and racial progress, his ideas influenced others for many years to come. For all of Washington's comments on manhood, and black manhood in particular, it was arguably black women who codified Washington's philosophy into a politics of respectability, which also included some of the very ideas championed by Du Bois.

The Politics of Respectability

Evelyn Brooks Higginbotham describes how black Baptist women came to see their race, gender, and religious identities as linked to slavery and the lasting impact of slavery on them and on others. Race is best understood, says Higginbotham, "as an unstable and decentered complex of meanings constantly being transformed by political struggle," which was derived "as the signifier of the master/slave relation thus emerged superimposed upon class and property relations" (1992, 256–257). The system of slavery, a system that dominated the lives of Abe Hawkins and others on Ashland Plantation, sanctioned "white ownership of black bodies and labor" (Higginbotham 1992, 257). Washington's address was calling for the continued ownership of black bodies and black labor, which appealed to white people hoping to maintain the function of slavery in the Southern economy, where the majority of black people were still living at the time of Washington's address through the first couple of decades of the twentieth century.

The continued ownership of black bodies and black labor was a source of frustration for many black people, including during the 1880s through the 1920s, which Higginbotham writes about. Black people, including black women were, like Washington, interested in racial progress and had their own ideas about what racial progress would look like and what it would require. The motto for the National Association of Colored Women (NACW) was "Lifting as We Climb." NACW was organized in Washington, DC, in response to disparaging comments about black women in a highly publicized letter by James Jacks, president of the Missouri Press Club, to a British antilynching society. The women were also inspired to organize because they wanted the right to vote and an end to the killings of black men by vigilante mobs, and segregation in public places, such as segregation in transportation. The women shared a general commitment to improving black life and thought that it was up to black women to do it.

The stereotypes associated with the enslaved and their descendants would only be removed if black women took the lead in disproving them. The route toward racial progress would include job training, equal pay, child care, an end to lynching and peonage, improved conditions in American prisons, criminal justice reform, and the integration of public transportation. NACW's agenda was viewed as reflecting an "elite attitude," because of the assertion that more affluent black people had a responsibility to help those "socially inferior." However, this is likely a misreading. It is clear to me that the so-called privileged black women did not see those economically struggling black women as biologically inferior but impacted by a host of social challenges and believed they had a religious and civic duty to make sure that everyone participates in upward social mobility. Evidence of this fact is the group's commitment to conduct voter registration drives and praise funds to establish schools, camps, and homes for the elderly that benefit black women regardless of their social class positions.

Just as Washington was criticized for his "policy of submission" and comments about black people rightfully beginning life at the bottom, so too were the women of the NACW for equating "normality with conformity to white middle-class models" (Higginbotham 1992, 271) and for focusing so much on race differences that a lack of significant attention was devoted to "intragroup social relation as relations of power" (Higginbotham 1992, 274).

The role of the black church cannot be underestimated in the development of the politics of respectability. Higginbotham said the black church was a place where black women found their own voice. Social and demographic changes that took place during the time of Washington's speech and onward prompted black women to organize their individual efforts to promote positive changes for black people, including black women. These changes included the massive movement of black people from the American South to the North and the West, employment prospects, consumerism, industrialization, the suffragist movement, and World War I.

In this safe space—the black church—black women reflected upon what Du Bois (1903) described as a double-consciousness. While Du Bois was referring to the challenge black people face in negotiating their racial identity and their identity as Americans, black women asserted the challenges associated with navigating their racial and gender identities. The black women responsible for developing the politics of responsibility joined together influenced by the Bible, racial self-help, Victorian ideology, and the principles in the US Constitution that were supposed to extend to black people, regardless of gender. The politics of respectability sat in "opposition to the social structures and symbolic representations of white supremacy" (Higginbotham 1992, 186).

The founders of the politics of respectability were convinced that individual reform was also key to racial progress as evidenced in the establishment of training schools for black women and girls. Changing behaviors and attitudes were viewed "both as a goal in itself and as a strategy for reform of the entire structural system of American race relations" (Higginbotham 1992, 187). Although Washington's views about racial progress and the pathways toward achieving it were conservative, to say the least, the politics of respectability was both conservative and radical, argued Higginbotham. The politics of respectability was meant to dismantle but reproduced "hegemonic values of white America" (Higginbotham 1992, 187). The politics of respectability "subverted and transformed the logic of race and gender subordination" (Higginbotham 1992, 188), while the sentiments in Washington's speech ignored black women altogether and supported the normalization of race subordination.

The politics of respectability was very powerful in its ability to counter the effects of "technologies of power" (Higginbotham 1992, 189). These technologies include films, books, and other forms of mass communication that demonized and disrespected black people, especially black women. Higginbotham described the "rhetoric of violence" reflected in these technologies that disseminated and normalized caricatures and stereotypes of black women (1992, 189).

While Washington's words created great divisions between conservative and radical black thinkers, the politics of respectability served and continues to serve as a bridge discourse, uniting people across arbitrary social categories. The politics of respectability also advocated black women and black men and black children working together for the improvement of the whole; Washington was much more concerned with advancing the interest of white people, including white people who gave financially to support his racial progress agenda. It was far easier to support someone like Washington who was advocating racial progress, on the one hand, and promising to maintain the racial status quo, on the other hand.

The politics of respectability did have what some described as a female version of Booker T. Washington in the person of Nannie Burroughs. Burroughs was heavily influenced but not controlled by her religious faith and tradition. Just as the "church of the slaves" served as a way to declare black people's human dignity during slavery, the church served a similar role for Burroughs and the millions of men and women she inspired. The absence of human dignity afforded to black people outlived the enslavement system. Booker T. Washington acknowledged the lack of human dignity for black people but he was more interested in racial reconciliation without respectability and accountability. The politics of respectability joined people like John Hope and W. E. B. Du Bois in demanding white people recognize the human dignity of black people.

Burroughs's religious faith was a liberating force as it has been for many other black people, but black liberation theory ignored black women for a time. She led the black Baptist women's movement from the early 1900s to the early 1960s. Her leadership and the politics of respectability reflected a "prophetic principle," which combined rewards in the hereafter with the "dream of human equality and human dignity in the America of their own time" (Brooks 1988, 12). The politics of respectability called for struggle against forces internal and external to the black race. Evelyn

Brooks (1988) found, her in article, "Religion, Politics, and Gender," that Burroughs blamed some black people for their own victimization and adopted a "behavior approach to racial progress" along a radical approach that sought to turn the racial social order on its head (1988, 113). Burroughs believed individual black people "had the power to confirm or refute racist stereotypes and racism in general," which essentially "privatized racial discrimination and rendered it less subject to government regulation, to the authority of the public realm" (Brooks 1988, 13).

It is important to acknowledge that Burroughs's perspective about the impact of individual behaviors on the entire black race, one that was and is still shared by other black people, is likely rooted in the fact that black people are and have been under constant surveillance by the dominate group for any opportunity to present or (re)present caricatures, stereotypes, and myths about black people. Hoping to remove the cloud of suspicion and to exert some form of agency, calls for behavior modification as a way to address racial discrimination is not illogical, although improbable and ill-informed. I contend that neither Burroughs nor anyone else espousing this viewpoint thought it was 100 percent foolproof, as experience had taught them that antiblack racism is in some ways unpredictable and in other ways very predictable. The evidence is clear that Nannie Burroughs and the National Association of Colored Women was not only focused on the "Bible, Bath, and the Broom," but on the racialized social system that has characterized American life during slavery and well beyond Burroughs's lifetime.

NACW worked with groups such as the National Association for the Advancement of Colored People (NAACP) to fight lynching. NACW supported antilynching legislation and raised awareness about the number of black women, in addition to the number of black men, victimized by lynch mobs. NACW, under the direction of Nannie Burroughs, also engaged in other forms of protests, including petitions and verbal protests.

NACW adopted list of demands at a 1913 meeting to address the needs of black people in the United States that did not involve individual behavior modifications. The list included:

1. Well-built, sanitary dwellings, and streets that are paved and kept just as clean as others in the town are kept

2. Equal accommodation on common carriers

3. Franchise for every Negro—North, South, East, and West— who is an intelligent and industrious citizen

4. Equal treatment in the courts

5. Equal division of school funds

6. Lynching stopped

7. Convict leasing system broken up and better prisons and humane treatment of Negro prisoners (Brooks 1988, 14–15)

NACW and Burroughs understood that racial progress would not come swiftly, but they did believe it would come and that it would come with persistent resistance. This was made clear when Burroughs "promised to continue to 'annoy' the railroads until facilities were upgraded" (Brooks 1988, 15). Burroughs and NACW challenged everyone—the political system, major corporations, black women, black men, white men, and white women—in their efforts to improve the lives of all black people. They pointed out the "hypocrisy of white reformers who advocated social purity for white women (Brooks 1988).

Garrett Duncan, in "Black Youth, Identity, and Ethics," wrote about the politics of responsibility and its impact on contemporary black youth. Duncan makes the case by arguing that most people view black culture as having "limited value in society and that it offers little in the way of social or psychological capital" (2005, 3). Analyzing identity models, Duncan explores the role of the ideology of respectability in shaping black youth identities. Respectability here is defined as an "ideology of middle-class morality that is intimately linked to white nationalism in Europe in the US" (Duncan 2005, 4). Duncan describes the stages of identity development, which are said to occur across three levels of awareness. These cognitive organizations, for Duncan (2005), include pre-encounter, where black people identify largely with the dominate culture; encounter occurs when black people are forced to confront the issue of race; and post-encounter is characterized by an appreciation and embracing of black cultural identity.

According to Duncan (2005), white middle-class morality became the standard in the late 1700s, early 1800s, and it involved the regulation of gender and social norms, including ideas about masculinity and a woman's place. Duncan's (2005) definition differs from the description of NACW in the notable absence of a focus on structural issues facing black people, although Duncan does state, "The conventional construction of black youth has been left largely to law enforcement agencies, social work and educational institutions, and popular culture" (2005, 5–6). Although

NACW and Burroughs fought against what Brooks (1988) describes as technologies of violence, Duncan found "these entities disseminate the received categories in society that depict black youth either as a social problem or as a mentally or emotionally debilitated social group (2005, 6). These entities viewed young black people as "beyond love" and outside the boundaries of respectability (Duncan 2005, 6), which is what the originators of the politics of respectability hoped to combat.

For Harriet published an interview with Evelyn Brooks Higginbotham and addressed the many ways in which scholars and the general public have misread and misunderstood the original meaning of the politics of respectability and the implications for examining racial progress, protests, and contemporary social movements.

In a recent interview, Higginbotham describes the politics of respectability as moral and centered upon self-determination. She attempts to answer the question, What is a life worthy of respect? For Higginbotham, the politics of respectability, as it was originally conceptualized and not as it has been reimagined, says, "I am worthy of respect. You don't respect me, but I'm worthy of respect."

The politics of respectability is not only applied to young black people or black women, but also to black athletes. Michael Vick, former quarterback for the Atlanta Falcons, made news when he suggested that Colin Kaepernick, former quarterback for the San Francisco 49ers and a most recognizable figure in recent protests against racial injustices during the playing of the national anthem at the start of NFL games, should go "clean cut" and abandon his Afro, which has long symbolized black protest, black power, and black identity, according to Tyler Tynes, author of "Colin Kaepernick, Michael Vick, and the Fallacy of Respectability Politics."

Racial Realism and the Myth of Racial Equality

For some scholars, and for many others, whether black people changing their attitudes, behaviors, and so forth, to fit so-called white middle-class standards will lead to improvements in their quality of life is not even up for debate, nor is the question about when and how to dismantle systemic racism. Among the foremost thinkers on this topic, and one of the key founders of critical race theory and racial realism, Derrick Bell proclaimed, "Racial equality is, in fact not a realistic goal" (1992a, 363). Racial equality "is unobtainable in a perilously racist America" (Bell 1992a, 363).

Far more people living during the life and times of Abe Hawkins, under the oppressive system of physical bondage, were likely to agree with Bell's outlook on the likelihood of racial progress than that set forth in the politics of respectability or in Washington's policy of submission. Abe Hawkins and his contemporaries likely placed little faith in the courts, although some black people enjoyed some success in the courts; nor does Bell, a legal scholar. The courts were not constructed to address the needs of black people. The purpose of the law and by extension the court, according to Bell, was "preserving the status quo and only periodically and unpredictably serving as a refuge of oppressed people" (1992a, 364).

Instead of focusing on racial equality, black people would do well to focus on racial realism, says Bell. Racial realism "is a legal and social mechanism on which blacks can rely to have their voice and outrage heard" (Bell 1992a, 364). Bell recounts the origins of racial realism. The perspective was influenced by legal realism. Legal realism focused on the function of law and not on the abstract conceptualization of the law. Legal realism changed how jurists and others understood the law "by exposing the result-oriented, value-laden nature of legal decision-making" (Bell 1992a, 368). Bell cites the *Bakke* case as a good example:

> Racism provides a basis for a judge to select one available premise rather than another when incompatible claims arise. An example presents itself in the case of *Regents of the University of California v. Bakke*. Relying heavily on the formalistic language of the Fourteenth Amendment, and utterly ignoring social questions about which race has been denied entry for centuries into academia, the court held that an affirmative action policy may not unseat white candidates on the basis of their race. (1992a, 369)

The case shows how formalists use abstractions to disguise the role of values in the formation of various judicial decisions and public policies.

Bell (1992a) is not the first black thinker to bemoan the likelihood of racial equality or question the merits of integration. As argued previously, Booker T. Washington did not advocate integration or racial equality. He commented on the inferiority of black people relative to white people and advocated for the separation of the races, particularly in all things social. Bell (1992a) explains what distinguishes racial realism from the policy of submission, physical bondage, and the politics of respectability. Bell acknowledges evidence that Washington privately supported initiatives that seemed to run counter to his public proclamations about black people and about what it would take for racial progress, but Washington's private support for such causes "could undo the damage of Washington's public pronouncement" (1992a, 371).

Bell (1992a) discusses other important moments in the history of the United States that highlight what he sees as the futility of focusing on racial equality, including the confirmation of Clarence Thomas, not only as a US Supreme Court justice, but as a "replacement" for the civil rights giant Thurgood Marshall (Bell 1992a, 371). In fact, Bell says the confirmation and appointment of Thomas "mark and mar the status of blacks well into the twenty-first century" (1992a, 371) as Washington did at the close of the nineteenth century. President George H. Bush's appointment of Thomas served as a "symbol of our powerlessness" in that President Bush elevated "one of us who is willing to denigrate and disparage all who look like him to gain favor, position, and prestige" (Bell 1992a, 370).

Furthermore, the confirmation of Clarence Thomas to the Supreme Court provided further proof or new evidence for some people about the shortcomings of the politics of respectability. Many highly educated, well-respected black scholars, black elected officials, black clergy, among others, were quite vocal in their disapproval of Bush's selection and their voices were not even considered. The refusal to acknowledge their concerns showed "that even the most accomplished blacks can be ignored with impunity when they seek to challenge an exercise of white, conservative power" (Bell 1992a, 371). The voices of black people who might otherwise serve as models for contemporary interpretations of the politics of respectability are easily neutralized by "well-meaning but confused blacks . . . who hoped for the best" (Bell 1992a, 372).

Thomas's confirmation was also significant because it was "both a reminder and a warning of the vulnerability of black rights and the willingness of powerful whites to sacrifice and subvert these rights in furtherance of political or economic ends (Bell 1992a, 373). The vulnerability of black rights is just one of many "acknowledged truths" (Bell 1992a, 373). It is a reality that even a racial optimist must concede. "All too many of the black people we sought to lift through law from a subordinate status to equal opportunity, are more deeply mired in poverty and despair than they were during the 'separate but equal era'" (Bell 1992a, 374). The "atmosphere of racial neutrality" (Bell 1992a, 374) and "reliance on racial remedies" (Bell 1992a, 375) are not good for black people. They merely serve as "mechanisms to make life bearable in a society where blacks are a permanent, subordinate class" (Bell 1992a, 377).

Bell calls on black people today to come to a realization that Abe Hawkins and other enslaved people came to during their lifetimes: "We must realize, as our slave forbearers, that the struggle for freedom is, at bottom, a manifestation of our humanity that survives and grows stronger through resistance to oppression, even if that oppression is never overcome" (Bell 1992a, 378).

Victor Erik Ray, Antonia Randolph, Megan Underhill, and David Luke (2017) collaborated on a review essay of various perspectives on racial perspectives including critical race theory, which was published in *Sociology of Race and Ethnicity*. The authors examine critical race theory, Afro-pessimism, and racial progress narratives. Ray and his colleagues (2017) argue that much of the sociology of race and ethnicity assumes a linear process characterized by slow improvement. The claim is surprising given the many published books and articles by sociologists who study race and ethnicity, especially black sociologists, who do view race and ethnicity in this manner. There are classical sociologists like W. E. B. Du Bois, for example, who did not see race in this manner, and contemporary sociologists who have used qualitative and quantitative methods to show that in many ways racial and ethnic disparities have worsened not improved over time.

Nevertheless, the authors go on to contrast sociology's racial optimism with the pessimism some see in critical race theory. Ray and his coauthors say critical race theory "sees progress as conflicted, contingent, and reversible" (Ray et al. 2017, 2). Ray and his colleagues do concede that both critical race theory and the sociology of race and ethnicity focus on "structural understandings of racial inequality," but the similarities appear to end there (2017, 2).

Afro-Pessimism and Modern-Day Slavery

Critical race theory, according to Ray et al. (2017), has some things in common with Afro-pessimism and critical theory, but there are also some key differences. Both critical race theory and Afro-pessimism share "skepticism about the racial progress narrative," but Afro-pessimism "insists upon the distinctiveness of anti-blackness from other forms of racism. Anti-blackness is the notion that the construction of blacks as non-human, structures the status of all other racial groups" (Ray et al. 2017, 3). More-over, Ray and his coauthors say Afro-pessimism resists calls for research on race to move beyond the historic black-white binary to include other racial groups: "Afro-pessimism replaces the binary between blacks and whites with an antagonism between blacks and non-blacks" (2017, 3). The authors seek to clarify any confusion there might be regarding the differences between anti-blackness and white supremacy. "Anti-blackness, not white supremacy, explains the social conditions of blacks across the globe" (Ray et al. 2017, 3).

Afro-pessimism is concerned with slavery and how slavery lives on today, say several of the founders, including Saidiya Hartman, Frank Wilderson, and Jared Sexton. Afro-pessimism says slavery changed form. Afro-pessimism defines the "meaning of whiteness as human (free, ratio-nal) developed in antagonism to the meaning of blackness as nonhuman (enslaved, incapable of reason" (Ray et al. 2017, 4). Another feature of Afro-pessimism is the "claim that slavery and the Middle Passage, through the experience of social death (permanent subjugations) gave blacks a different ontology than other racial groups" (Ray et al. 2017, 4), which the scholars claim is new but may be found in sociological works on race and ethnicity published in the past. The three characteristics that Afro-pessimists say define slavery as social death include: natal alienation, gratuitous violence, and social dishonor (Ray et al. 2017, 4).

Frank Wilderson III, according to James Zug, author of "The Italicized Life of Frank Wilderson '78," is without question one of the main architects of Afro-pessimism (2010). Afro-pessimism started in the mid-1990s with a symposium organized by Wilderson and Sexton. Afro-pessimism fills an important gap in scholarly work on race by recognizing the need to place theories into a particular historical context, declares Jared Sexton. Afro-pessimism is heavily influenced by scholars concerned with the idea of the human, writes James Zug. For proponents of Afro-pessimism, black people are regarded as nonhuman, without familial connections, and subject to terror, exploitation, and violence without just cause (Zug 2010).

Frank Wilderson uses the term "prison-slave-in-waiting" to describe "an ordinary Black person" (2003b, 19). He describes "Black citizenship, or Black civic obligation," as oxymoronic (Wilderson 2003b, 19) because "for black people, civil society *itself*—rather than its abuses or shortcomings—is a state of emergency" (Wilderson 2003b, 19). For Wilderson, there is a clear "absence of the Black subject" (2003b, 22).

The focus for Afro-pessimism is not on racial equality but on violence. A focus on violence allows for the debunking of myths around accepted philosophical assumptions "because violence not only makes thought possible, but it makes black metaphysical being and black rationality impossible, while simultaneously giving rise to the philosophical contemplation of metaphysics and thick description of human relation" (Douglass and Wilderson 2013, 117). The very essence of blackness, according to Afro-pessimism, "is constituted by violence with no event horizons" (Douglass and Wilderson 2013, 117).

Slavery was not merely a time period for R. L.; rather, slavery is characterized by racial domination. The black subject merely ceased being a slave with respect to a master and became a slave to his or her appearance, contends R. L. The structural position of the slave made the white elite possible. Slaves were, by design, outside the boundaries of humanity, which is equated with whiteness, says R. L. (2013).

R. L. links contemporary policing with slave patrols and relates both to white supremacy. Slave patrols regulated mobility as slaves were tied directly to plantations, while policing regulates movements of blacks according to various forms of spatial configurations (2013). In the case of slave patrols and policing, space was racialized. The exercise of police power is among the practices.

Afro-pessimism has supporters and critics. Some scholars are not convinced that the "condition of Black life in the modern era is . . . simply a nuanced recodification of the original violence of the plantation" (Barlow 2016, 1). A more general critique of Afro-pessimism is the absence of a link between theory and application (Barlow 2016, 1). Sexton acknowledges that some criticize Afro-pessimism for a so-called rejection of agency.

Resistance and Free Agency:
From Abe Hawkins to Colin Kaepernick

Debates about what racial progress looks like and debates about whether or not racial progress is even possible will likely continue for the foreseeable future. What is clear is that some people, including some black people, have committed to or recommitted to efforts to resist private actions and public policies that disadvantage black people and other people of color, while others have not. Athletes, like Colin Kaepernick are great examples of a commitment to shine a light on racial injustices in America. Adaptive activist-athletes, including Kaepernick, have demonstrated not only a renewed commitment to civic engagement, but also a commitment to the exercise of their agency and highlight the limits of racial progress in America.

The events of the summer of 2016 had a particularly significant impact on Kaepernick and his supporters. On August 14, 2016, and August 20, 2016, Colin Kaepernick refused to stand during the playing of the national anthem and no one really paid attention. Kaepernick sat again on August 26, 2017, which caught the attention of a reporter. A few weeks prior to the protests two black men, Alton Sterling and Philando Castile, were killed at the hands of law enforcement officials and their deaths were recorded and shared widely.

Alton Sterling, according to the Associated Press (2017), was a thirty-seven-year-old father of five and resident of Baton Rouge. He was well known in his community. He was shot at close range while on the ground in front of Triple S Food Mart on the corner of Fairfields Avenue and North Foster Drive. Officers Blane Salamoni and Howie Lake II were said to be responding to a report of someone with a gun threatening people outside of the store around 12:30 a.m. Salamoni was on the Baton Rouge Police Department (BRPD) for four years at the time of the shooting and Lake was on the force for just three years. Both officers had complaints against them for prior use of force. The officers were equipped with body cameras. According to the BRPD, the body cameras fell off in the encounter with Alton Sterling. The actual shooting was captured on two cell phone videos. The officers contend Alton Sterling did not comply with their instructions. They also claim they saw the butt of a gun in Sterling's pocket and that Sterling reached for the gun as they struggled on the ground. Sterling was tasered more than once, said Greg Allen and Kelly McEvers (2017) in transcripts from *All Things Considered* and from reports by the Associated Press (2017). Allen and McEvers also report that Alton Sterling was shot at least three times in his back.

The city of Baton Rouge, and cities across the country, erupted in protests. Many people were arrested in the protests and even filed legal action against the police department, based upon reporting by Chris Sommerfeldt. A settlement was reached between the city and the protesters in the amount of $100,000. Each one of the ninety-two plaintiffs is expected to receive about $230 each. The protesters accused officers of being too aggressive, using unconstitutional methods, and hindering their rights to freedom of speech and the right to assemble peacefully, argues Sommerfeldt (2016). The protesters, including some closely associated with the national #BlackLivesMatter movement, were originally charged with obstructing a roadway and engaging in disorderly conduct. While the overwhelming majority of the city's Metro Council voted in support of the settlement, Metro councilmember John Delgado voted against it because he believed such settlements "encourage protesters to act recklessly in the future" and expressed "no interest in paying $100,000 in taxpayer dollars to people who are coming into our city to protest." Delgado ignored the violation of the protesters' rights. He describes the actions of the activists as reckless and not that of the officers in question or the officers involved in the shooting that prompted the protests to begin with. As in the past, Delgado claimed that protesters are so-called outside agitators, which implies good race relations between black and white people in Baton Rouge.

Another important development that followed the killing of Alton Sterling, protests, and the ambush of law enforcement officials a short time later was the passage of what is referred to as the Blue Lives Matter law and similar laws in other states.

More than a dozen states introduced bills to include police officers in hate crime laws despite the fact that all fifty states have laws that make killing a police officer punishable by death without a stated motive, which is the signature of hate crime laws. The proposals and laws call into question the motivations behind the introduction of the legislation, and the passing of the legislation in at least one state—Louisiana. Julia Craven (2017), writing about Blue Lives Matter laws, says the bills and new law expose "an appetite to provide political sanctuary to an already protected class." Craven reports that some activists describe the moves as "counterproductive, creating deeper divisions between police and the communities they serve." Moreover, people against the bills and the law contend "that including police in hate crime laws is merely a political statement and an unnecessary one at that." Collier Meyerson (2016), the author of "The Case Against 'Blue Lives Matter' Bills," reporting on the problems associated with the bills and the law, said they were vague and "at their core, Blue Lives Matter bills . . . seek to turn Black Lives Matter protesters into enemies of the state."

Just as the killing of Alton Sterling shocked the Baton Rouge community, the nation, and the world, the killing of a young, beloved, cafeteria worker also had a lasting impact on police killings and responses to them. The killing of Philando Castile by Jeronimo Yanez occurred a day after the killing of Alton Sterling in Minnesota. Castile was riding in a car with his girlfriend and her four-year-old daughter. Yanez shot Castile shortly after Philando Castile informed him that he had a weapon and Castile's girlfriend broadcast the aftermath of the shooting on Facebook live, reports Steve Karnowski (2017). With total disregard for the safety of the young girl or the humanity of anyone in the vehicle, Yanez ended the life of a beloved member of his community. Like many other officer-involved shootings, Yanez was not found guilty of second-degree manslaughter in the killing of Philando Castile, reports Nick Visser (2017) in an article, "5 Disturbing Statements by the Cop Who Shot Philando Castile." Yanez was encouraged to leave the force, did so, and received a buyout in the amount of at least $48,500, acknowledges Amy Forlitit (2017), author of "The Police Officer Who Shot Philando Castile Will Be Paid $48,500 in a Buyout."

Sadly, Alton Sterling and Philando Castile were only two of the nearly 260 people killed by police during the year Kaepernick started his protest. Of the at least 258 people killed by police in 2016, 39 were unarmed, 4 died after the use of stun guns, and 9 died in custody, reports Julia Craven (2017). Most of the black people killed by police were shot to death. According to published reports, about one-third of the unarmed people killed in 2016 were black men, although black men only make up about 6 percent of the population. It is not hard to see how Kaepernick and others were motivated to do something even if they were not sure that their particular actions would lead to transformative changes.

Colin Kaepernick was careful to keep the focus where it ought to be—on the unjust killings of Alton Sterling and Philando Castile and other examples of racial injustice, although many people from fans, owners, even the president of the United States tried to direct attention elsewhere. Martin and McHendry, authors of "Kaepernick's Stand: Patriotism, Protest, and Professional Sports," write about how even some of Kaepernick's supporters made the protests more about Kaepernick's right to protest as opposed to ongoing racial injustices. In a relatively short time there were lots of conversations about "the culture of compulsory patriotism" (Martin and McHendry 2016, 88). It seemed as if there were people from the stadium seats to the front office demanding Kaepernick not only stand during the anthem but also explain his stance.

Martin and McHendry cite remarks made by Kelly Crigger, a retired colonel in the United States Army, as representative of the aforementioned sentiment. Crigger remarked, "You're not a freedom fighter leading people out of bondage. You're an ill-informed athlete who's only fanning the fires of racism by sitting on the sidelines for a principle that you only understand through a simplistic pop narrative that's little more than a hashtag campaign" (Martin and McHendry 2016, 89–90).

Crigger, like many who oppose Kaepernick and #BlackLivesMatter, see no connection between slavery and the current state of race relations in America. He implies that black people attained freedom when slavery ended, as if there aren't examples of the continued subordination of black people since slavery ended. Crigger also views Kaepernick through the "dumb jock" narrative when he describes him as ill-informed. He also sees racism as something that is not normative and part of the very fabric of American life but as something that arises or disappears depending at the whim of people seeking to create problems where none exists. Crigger also seeks to minimize and discount the reality of the conditions that prompted Kaepernick's protest and did not miss an opportunity to associate him with a movement that some Americans, mainly white Americans, view at best as a group of racial ambulance chasers and at worse as a terrorist group, like in the report by Tom Kertscher (2017) in "Pro-Sheriff David Clarke Group Says Clarke Called Black Lives Matter Hate Group, Terrorist Movement."

In their analysis of reactions to Kaepernick's protest, Martin and McHendry view these defense strategies as "efforts to control the means of protest" that "ultimately end up silencing marginalized populations from voicing any discontent at all" (2016, 98). Criticisms of Kaepernick's protest drew a response from President Donald J. Trump, who suggested NFL owners should fire anyone who does not stand for the anthem. The tone of the president's comments and comments by NFL owners brightened the spotlight on the protests—if not on the issue of racial inequality in America—and led the NFL owners to develop a plan that would include donations to nonprofit organizations as a demonstration of their commitment to addressing some of the challenges Kaepernick wanted to draw attention to, writes Ken Belson (2017) of the *New York Times*. However, the NFL owner's proposal was not supported by some players and smelled of philanthrocapitalism or socially responsible capitalism in which elite whites give money to causes to address challenges from which they benefit or helped create, terms described in the work of Zenia Kish and Justin Leroy (2015). NFL owners benefit from the structures that spatially isolated people of color and low-income people and limited their opportunities so much so that they view sports, such as professional football, as one of the very few legitimate opportunities for social mobility. NFL owners are often tied to the corporations, elected officials, and most importantly ideologies that perpetuate the structural racial inequalities that persist in American society.

Some people, including Kaepernick supporters, thought the standout quarterback could do more than kneel. Kaepernick was challenged to use his status and resources to address some of the challenges facing communities of color. Kaepernick responded not by throwing money at "the problem" and donating to organizations with recognizable names, such as the United Negro College Fund, but by giving to a host of grassroots organizations working to transform individuals, families, and communities, says Greg Bishop and Ben Baskin (2017) writing for *Sports Illustrated*.

GQ magazine named Colin Kaepernick Citizen of the Year. The magazine elected Kaepernick believing he risked everything to change society, putting him in the rare company of people like Muhammad Ali, John Carlos, and Tommie Smith. The editors of *GQ* (2017), stating why Kaepernick was selected, note there are ninety quarterbacks in the NFL and Kaepernick, easily better than at least seventy of them, still has not be been signed to a team. He is not playing because of any career injury but because he dared draw attention to racial injustices in America in uniform. He dared to challenge the football establishment from one of the most powerful positions on the field—one that was off-limits for people that looked like him for much of the league's history. Kaepernick resisted in a number of ways, from kneeling to wearing his hair in such a way as to make his racial and political identity hypervisible.

Adaptive Leadership and New Social Movements

Colin Kaepernick's personal protest mobilized others to tackle the tough challenge that is racial inequality in America. Kaepernick represents a new generation of leadership who see leaders not as people who occupy positions of authority but as a practice open to anyone and any moment in time.

Ronald Heifetz, Alexander Grashow, and Marty Linsky define adaptive leadership as "the practice of mobilizing people to tackle tough challenges and thrive" (2009, 2). The goal of adaptive leadership is to have a positive social impact. Adaptive leadership builds on the past and involves experimentation. Adaptive leadership relies on diversity and seeks to significantly displace, reregulate, and rearrange, argue Heifetz and his coauthors. Those engaged in the practice of leadership understand that adaptive change takes time and that systems are not broken but operate in the way that people benefiting from the systems want them to function. There is no crisis. Systems are structured in such a way as to yield the outcomes they get, say, Heifetz, Grashow, and Linsky.

Adaptive leaders are not popular and should not anticipate support because "no one who tries to name or address the dysfunction in an organization (or in a country) will be popular" (Heifetz, Grashow, and Linsky 2009, 5). People in positions of power prefer "the current situation to trying something new where the consequences are unpredictable and likely to involve loses to key parties" (Heifetz, Grashow, and Linsky 2009, 5). Those key parties must be willing to change their loyalties, priorities, beliefs, and habits, say Heifetz and his colleagues. Clearly, changing laws did not erase racial disparities in America, in part because changing laws to achieve racial equality and/or to see racial progress represents a technical solution to an adaptive challenge.

Adaptive leadership requires an understanding of the difference between technical and adaptive challenges. Both Kaepernick and Hawkins understood the difference between technical and adaptive problems and the type of responses that each required.

Ronald Heifetz, Alexander Grashow, and Marty Linsky describe technical problems as problems that "can be solved applying existing know-how and the organization's current problem-solving processes" (2009, 2). As elite athletes, Kaepernick and Hawkins surely knew how to make changes to improve their performances. "Adaptive problems, on the other hand, require individuals . . . to alter their ways . . . as the people themselves are the problem, the solution lies with them" (Heifetz, Grashow, and Linsky 2009, 2). Kaepernick's desire to address the problem of racial inequality in America could not be fixed with a technical fix in part because some people did not see racial inequality as a problem. Kaepernick's adaptive response was to raise awareness about racial inequality and provoke people in positions of power to work toward the creation of a more equitable society. Similarly, Abe Hawkins and the hundreds of slaves on Ashland Plantation understood that freedom for them would not come were it simply up to slave owners and other beneficiaries of the enslavement system, but an end of slavery would require individuals to change their ways and demand that institutions change too. Hawkins and others knew that real progress requires "those who lead to ask themselves and the people to select a solution that may require turning part or all of the organization upside down" (Heifetz, Grashow, and Linsky 2009, 2)

Kaepernick and Hawkins were both change makers in the tradition of adaptive leadership. Heifetz and colleagues warn that change makers "may be attacked directly in an attempt to shift the debate to your character and style to avoid discussion of the issue" (2009, 3). There are many examples of attacks on Kaepernick's character and style from people like Michael Vick to the retired army colonel to the president of the United States. Abe Hawkins, one of the most successful jockeys of his era, was accused of throwing a race. The fact that Abe Hawkins, a man regarded by most as honest and of good character when very few positive things were said about black people, points to Hawkins as someone who sought to effectuate changes on and off the track.

There is a reason that NFL owners, plantation owners, among others, would assault the character of change makers like Kaepernick and Hawkins. "By attempting to undercut you, people strive to restore order, maintain what is familiar to them, and protect themselves from the pains of adaptive change. They want to be comfortable again and you're in the way" (Heifetz, Grashow, and Linsky 2009, 4). Heifetz and colleagues add, "When the status quo is upset, people feel a sense of profound loss and dashed expectations. They may go through a period of feeling incompetent or disloyal. It's no wonder they resist the change or try to eliminate its visible agent" (2009, 5).

Conclusion

Kaepernick's protest is part of a larger discussion involving black intellectuals and black people about whether racial progress is possible and how best to achieve it. Colin Kaepernick and his supporters clearly rejected Booker T. Washington's policy of submission, while embracing W. E. B. Du Bois's commitment to immediate social justice in all areas of life. Colin Kaepernick rejected the idea that one's appearance had to meet the white, middle-class standards Evelyn Brooks Higginbotham described but embraced the black Baptist women's commitment to social justice issues. Kaepernick is clearly a racial realist in the tradition of Derrick Bell, recognizing that working through the courts is not the most effective strategy for bringing about social change. Like Frank Wilderson III, Kaepernick understands the linkages between contemporary black athletes and their enslaved predecessors.

Irrespective of Kaepernick's concerns that his actions might not lead to immediate societal changes, he demonstrated his agency, and in doing so, mobilized other black athletes that there is power in the fight. He also showed that leadership was not about a position one occupied, but a practice. Kaepernick's protest continues the modern-day movement where black people, from athletes to ordinary citizens, feel empowered to resist an unjust system while some black scholars and black elected officials have seemingly turned away.

Colin Kaepernick demonstrated the same courage and bravery that people committed to narrowing the gap between society as it is and society as it ought to be have demonstrated for hundreds of years, irrespective of the political climate. Debates about whether racial progress is linear, incremental, and inevitable as opposed to unobtainable are ongoing with no resolution in sight. What is clear is that contemporary athletes are following Kaepernick's lead and stepping in the footprints of other black athletes willing to use their favored—albeit tenuous—status to draw attention to issues that far too many Americans wish to ignore, namely, illuminating persistent racial disparities. Kaepernick embodies a commitment to mobilizing others to effectuate change in their own corners of the world in the way that works best for them. The takeaway from Kaepernick's actions is that we all are empowered to engage in the practice of leadership and have a responsibility to use our resources— whether modest or vast—to bequeath to the next generation a nation more just than the one we inherited.

Changing Course

Race-Transcendent Prophets Must Lead the Way

Far too many Americans have arrived at the conclusion that efforts to adequately compensate black people for the discrimination they faced (and continue to face) are unfair to present-day white people and/or "politically unfeasible" and are, therefore, not worth the fight. White privilege, some argue, is not experienced equally by whites, as evidenced in variations in outcomes by gender, for example. Moreover, poor white people, regardless of gender, and more affluent whites have little in common, others have claimed.

The idea of white disadvantaged extends further; it extends to the idea that white people are actually one of the most at-risk groups in America. White people are believed to be at-risk due to perceived black progress, external threats ranging from terrorism to illegal immigration, among other claims. The belief that whites are at-risk has seemingly increased over the past decade and has politically energized many white Americans, including around such themes as Make America Great Again.

The consequences of these developments are many and are not limited to upticks in overt manifestations of white supremacy, such as in the case

Portions of the conclusion were previous published in the following publication: Lori Latrice Martin, "American (Un)Civil Religion, the Defense of the White Worker, and Responses to NFL Protests," in *The Religion of White Rage: Religious Fervor, White Workers and the Myth of Black Racial Progress*, edited by Stephen C. Finley, Biko Mandela Gray, and Lori Latrice Martin (Edinburgh: Edinburgh University Press, 2020).

of the burning of historic black churches, but also include a potentially dangerous and harmful decline in commitments to speak truth to power when the issue is 1) clearly about race and 2) involves the experiences of black people in America.

Various groups ranging from white liberals to selected black scholars and black politicians are among the former freedom fighters that have seemingly retreated from talking about race in discourses related to differences between black and white people. Some former advocates for the rights of historically disadvantaged groups appear to have to become proponents of programs and proposals that defy history, logic, and hundreds of years of scholarly research and embrace the existence or emergence of a race-fair America. This is due, at least in part, to white backlash.

Black people continue to bear the brunt of the blame for enduring racial disparities in virtually every area of social life from wealth, education, health, to crime. Efforts claiming to address such issues, particularly those adhering to the idea of a race-fair America, tend to focus on the pathology of blackness, which is rooted in antiblack sentiment. Consequently, solutions to racial disparities call for behavior modifications that will lead to conformity with mythical so-called white, middle-class standards. At the same time, current solutions to racial disparities also direct attention away from the need for systemic changes and the need for the erasure of antiblack sentiments from both the American psyche and social fabric.

In this book, I argued that the road to a race-fair America is paved with universal programs that are: 1) focused primarily on behavioral modifications, 2) open to all, and 3) benefit the common good. I identified a number of problems with this line of thinking.

First, I showed that the root of America's race problem is the systematic exclusion of black people in all areas of social life. Second, I argued that the term *common* was never meant to and still does not include black people. Next, I highlighted the fact that the material and nonmaterial harm done to black peoples is still felt today, must be acknowledged, and just compensation is long overdue. Moreover, the idea that programs that are available to all people will necessarily benefit black people has been shown not to always be the case.

Millions of black people have been in (and are still caught in) a disadvantage feedback loop, whereby generations of black people suffer the effects of antiblack practices and policies. These practices and policies tend to enrich members of the dominant racial group both literally and figuratively. This exploitation and exclusion is not new, but it is a fact some wish to forget, or chose to ignore for reasons unknown. Doing what is right is not something that any individual or group should give up so easily.

America in Denial examined the myth of a race-fair America by examining the danger done (and the potential for additional harm) of universal programs and policies, as well as other allegedly race-neutral initiatives claiming to positively impact the plights of black people in America. I considered asset building, education, and criminal justice.

In *America in Denial* I argued that addressing race-neutral practices and policies is both important and timely. I contended that the belief that America is moving more toward a colorblind society is likely growing and the next phase of that perspective is the idea of a race-fair America. Many people with influence and power, from political candidates to local elected officials to scholars, are promoting race-neutral policies. The (mis) use of black scholars, in particular, provides cover for elected officials and presidential hopefuls needed to garner support and authenticity required to increase public support for their initiatives. *America in Denial* met the need to unpack and debunk these issues and addressed a need to place them in appropriate historical contexts. Alternatives to potentially harmful universal, race-neutral policies and programs must be part of the conversation.

One need only look at the COVID-19 pandemic for evidence of the significance of accounting for race and creating appropriate policies that seriously consider the racial differences in the health and economic impact on black people relative to other groups. The number of people infected with COVID-19 is not known due to a host of factors, including the inability to test people. What is known is the number of hospitalizations and the number of deaths due to COVID-19. According to the World Health Organization (2020), as of April 17, 2020, there were more than 716,000 confirmed COVID-19 cases. While nearly 60,000 people recovered from virus, more than 33,000 died. The number of confirmed cases and deaths, for example, varied by state. In New York, there were over 222,000 confirmed COVID-19 cases, as of April 17, 2020, and over 14,600 deaths. There were over 30,000 confirmed cases in Michigan and about 2,200 deaths. Louisiana reported more than 21,500 confirmed cases of COVID-19 and over 1,000 deaths.

A recent article in the *Washington Post* reported that the in United States, as of April 16, 2020, more than twenty million Americans applied for unemployment assistance after Trump declared a national emergency on March 13, 2020. Heather Long (2020), the author of the article, stated that the United States has not experienced job losses of this magnitude since the Great Depression. The economic impact of the pandemic in America was felt across all sectors, including manufacturing and new home construction, according to the report from Long (2020).

Until recently, race was not part of the national conversations about COVID-19. However, many scholars who study race understand that in good times or bad times, most nonwhite people in America are less well-off than members of the dominant group and as a consequence perpetually endangered, vulnerable, and at risk when members of the dominant racial group experience a natural or human disaster (Bell 1992a and 1992b; Frazier 1957; Massey and Denton 1993). This has historically been the case for black people in America. Consequently, it is not surprising that in many states with the highest number of COVID-19 confirmed cases and deaths, black people are overrepresented among those dead and dying (Ray 2020). In Louisiana, according to a report from *Brookings*, 70 percent of COVID-19 deaths in Louisiana were black residents (Perry, Harsbarger, and Romer 2020). Black people only make up one-third of the total population of the state. In Chicago, black people make up 29 percent of the population but by mid-April accounted for 70 percent of COVID-19 deaths (Perry, Harsbarger, and Romer 2020). In Washington, DC, where black people make up 46 percent of the population, they made up over 62 percent of the deaths (Perry, Harsbarger, and Romer 2020). Black deaths due to COVID-19 in Detroit, Michigan, account for almost 85 percent of the state's COVID-19 deaths (Perry, Harsbarger, and Romer 2020).

As has been the case in the past, nonwhites are often scapegoated or blamed when members of the dominant group experience any number of hardships. In the case of the COVID-19 pandemic, Trump regularly referred to the virus as the "Chinese virus" (Somvichian-Clausen 2020). He routinely blamed China for not warning the United States about the severity of the COVID-19 outbreak in that country. Efforts to get the president to admit that the federal government was ill-prepared for the pandemic and failed to respond adequately were regularly deflected with negative remarks about China and the so-called Chinese virus. Hate crimes and other anti-Asian acts reportedly increased after Trump's remarks (Somvichian-Clausen 2020).

The current administration appeared mystified at the racial disparities in COVID-19 deaths despite the existence of racial health disparities on the leading causes of death (Hammonds and Reverby 2019). Black people are more likely than other groups to have significant health challenges and often experience more negative outcomes as a consequence, including death (Hammonds and Reverby 2019). As we have seen with COVID-19, efforts to explain racial disparities tend to focus on individuals and presumed pathological behaviors and not on the systems and structures that create and recreate conditions where racial differences exist, leaving some groups to thrive while others are literally left to die (Harris et al. 2015). Moreover, there is widespread speculation that both black workers and black businesses will be hit harder by the economic effects of COVID-19. Many minority-owned businesses are not expected to benefit from bailouts for small businesses due to such factors as their limited access to large financial institutions responsible for administering the finite funds. Black workers and black businesses were lagging behind their white counterparts before the global pandemic. It is important that any short-term and long-term efforts to mitigate the negative impact of COVID-19 on Americans must address persistent racial disparities.

In the introduction to *America in Denial: How Race-Neutral Policies Reinforce Racial Inequality in America*, I explored the causes and consequences of racial disparities in America and the various ways that ordinary citizens and scholars, particularly black scholars, have attempted to use their expertise to explain the structural underpinnings of racial disparities on a host of sociological outcomes for the purpose of improving the economic, political, and social standing of black people in America. I also highlighted some of the reasons some individuals are retreating from the fight for the ongoing black liberation struggle.

In the chapter "The Road to a Race-Fair America: How America Lost Its Way," I explored the rise of colorblind rhetoric as a means to downplay the role of race in America. In this chapter I also addressed the ways in which factors other than race, such as class, have been used in an attempt to debunk the idea that race is still the most significant determinant for black people in America.

In "Wealth, Inclusivity, and Exclusion," I explored racial disparities in the types and levels of assets owned. The causes and consequences of persistent racial wealth disparities and black asset poverty were discussed. Popular programs aimed at addressing the racial wealth gap were reviewed with special attention devoted to Individual Development Accounts (IDA), baby bonds, and reparations. I showed how universal programs will do little, if anything, to address the racial wealth gap and will surely not lead to a race-fair America. Contributions from largely public sources are relatively small and come with a number of strings attached. Funds may only be used in limited ways, such as for the purchase of a home or for a business venture, for example. The programs ignore the relatively low return on investments that black people receive from such assets when compared with white people in America. Previous research related to topics such as racial capitalism, philanthrocapitalism, and financial instruments as technologies of antiblackness were also reviewed and analyzed. They inform the ways in which the programs identified may be understood as paternalistic and reflect a hypersurveillance of black bodies through state-sponsored biometric registries. Many of the programs do not go far enough to narrow the racial wealth gap between black and white people in the United States.

"From Compulsory Education to Universal Disappointment" debunked the idea that education is the great equalizer. I showed that little has changed since the landmark *Brown v. Board of Education of Topeka, Kansas*, in that many schools are as segregated now as they were decades ago. Public schools, which are accessible to all, are underresourced and feeders to what scholars have called the school-to-prison pipeline. Universal pre-K programs claim to benefit black people whose children have historically had limited access to such programs, relative to white people, but evidence of racial disparities is evidenced here as shown in initiatives aimed at addressing the educational challenges of black youths from the cradle through college. In this chapter I also examined literature that exposes the linkages between educational attainment, race, and the wealth gap. I addressed a number of recent trends that further exacerbate problems associated with calls for universal community college, or college-for-all programs. These trends include historical declines in enrollment of black students and the dismal numbers of black graduate students and faculty. Claims of commitments to and the value of diversity, notwithstanding, education, including universal and/or race-neutral policies and programs, is not the only way, or even the best way, to a race-fair America.

Racial disparities in the criminal justice system are apparent from decisions about policing strategies to arrests to prosecutions, which I explored in the chapter "The Color of Justice." I argued that programs and policies aimed at addressing violent crimes, curbing gang activities, and addressing quality of life issues are framed in such a way as to convince the public that they are race neutral and intended for the common good. Agents of the criminal justice system are also viewed as race neutral and thus virtually immune from criminal prosecution in cases, for example, involving a black civilian and a white police officer. Current policing strategies and criminal justice reforms aimed at addressing mass incarceration do not apply equally to all, nor are they experienced in the same way by all, and will not lead to a race-fair America.

In the chapter "Resistance and Racial Progress: Kaepernick and the Practice of Leadership," I included a discussion about what it looks like to fight back against race neutrality and the risks change makers face. I showed that sports are not just a source of entertainment. Sports are part of a larger industrial complex. Sports are a social institution and impacted by many of the *-isms* impacting the broader society, including racism. I addressed the *shut up and play* sentiment aimed at professional athletes, like Colin Kaepernick. I showed that what is needed is more people like Kaepernick, who refused to wait for a more politically feasible time to draw attention to critical social problems and paid a great price.

One of the greatest issues is in how various Americans define *race fair*. For far too many white people in America, a race-fair America involves ignoring, minimizing, or delegating historical and contemporary harms to blacks and denying them the benefits afforded to members of the dominant racial group. It involves explaining away racial disparities as the result of the prevalence of a deviant black culture and willing lack of adherence to preferred white dominant norms and values. For many others, including many black people in America, a race-fair America involves understanding the necessity of taking account of race historically and in contemporary times as the most significant factor in black/white differences on a variety of outcomes related to wealth, education, and criminal justice. It also includes a demand for appropriate redress.

While the nation has lost its way, moving away from its core values as they relate to interactions with black people, it must be willing to change course. The directional change must move beyond the mere rhetoric of diversity and inclusion. It is not enough to merely change how the nation and its institutions look and do nothing about how they operate.

The time for doing what is right is now. There has never been a completely politically feasible time for addressing a number of critical issues, especially given the partisan nature of the nation's two-party system. To be clear, partisan divides, which are always informed by race, may be heightened at times when elected leaders seek to capitalize on antiblack sentiments to further their own political careers and/or to inflate their already inflated sense of self-importance.

Some of the most influential American thinkers challenged the racial status quo at great risk to their physical well-being and their professional careers, among other sacrifices. People like Martin Luther King Jr., Malcolm X, Toni Morrison, Angela Davis, Eduardo Bonilla-Silva, Ida B. Wells, W. E. B. Du Bois, and countless others, are among the great black intellectual thinkers who refused to allow rampant lynchings and the incarceration of conscientious objectors prevent them from centering the experiences of black people and forcing America to reconcile what the nation claims to value and how it actually treats black people within its borders.

These race-transcendent prophets are sorely needed today, as are so-called white liberals who do not just articulate an understanding of racial disparities or engage in never-ending dialogues about race. White liberals must get off the sidelines and do more than post and tweet about racial injustices, knowing full well the potential risks. As King and others have noted, doing nothing is the same as doing something. The relative silence of liberal whites is akin to their joining forces with the tiki torch–carrying white people who fail to see racial disparities as a problem created by the dominant racial group, a group they claim to abhor. Choosing the path of least resistance emboldens the many white people who see themselves as the victims of an oppressive system. They mistakenly view black people as winning at the expense of white people. The perceived victimization of white people is harming black people and perpetuating myths about the causes and consequences of racial disparities in America.

What is needed are more race-transcendent prophets. Race-transcendent prophets, according to scholar Cornel West, wed struggle and dignity regardless of the costs (Martin 2019). These prophets are needed in the so-called Ivory Tower, in the White House, in the halls of Congress, in news outlets, and every corner of the country. What is needed are more people willing to stand behind history and not hate to reveal the true sources of racial inequality in America.

To understand how race-transcendent prophets compare to other groups more fully, I argue it is important to consider the relationship between support for race-neutral strategies, degree of race consciousness, and adherence to American civil religion.

Race Fairness, Race Consciousness, and the Belief in American Civil Religion: A Matter of Intensity

Responses to perceived black progress by members of the dominant group in America have created the climate that some have characterized as politically unfeasible for strategies that are race conscious. Part of the resistance and backlash against race-conscious strategies to address enduring racial disparities can be explained by efforts on the part of members of the dominant group to (re)affirm American civil religion, which I discussed earlier in the book. The intensity of the reactions to perceived black programs and/or proposed race-conscious strategies varies. Variations in the reactions to perceived black progress and race-conscious initiatives point to the complexity associated with adherence to American civil religion and to one's level of race consciousness. To that end, I created a typology including the following types: white priestly preservationists, well-meaning whites, race contrarians, and race-transcendent prophets. It is important to note that these types are not necessarily mutually exclusive. The types are fluid and may vary by context, place, and time, for example. I also wish to provide further comments about my use of the term *race consciousness* here. High race consciousness refers to the extent to which black people identify with the historical struggle for social justice for that group and understand that what happens to black people as a group effects what happens to them as individuals. The opposite is true for black people with low race consciousness. White people with low race consciousness refuse to, or fail to, acknowledge the unearned benefits they receive based upon their race and are threatened by perceived black progress. White people with high race consciousness have a greater awareness about the role of race in the American social structure and may acknowledge at least some of the ways in which they benefit because of their membership in the dominant race in America.

White priestly preservationists have low race consciousness and high adherence to American civil religion. The type includes white workers fearful of racial progress and demonstrating intense white religious shock and white fervor under the guise of preserving their individual and national heritage. White workers brandishing divisive symbols, such as the Confederate flag, tiki torches, and white nationalist apparel are examples of white priestly preservationists and are arguably the most likely to demonstrate their white rage in a variety of forms, including physical assaults on nonwhite groups as well as the consumption and participation in of social media to harass and intimidate those critical of their beliefs, including black elected officials, black professors critical of whiteness, and other people of color.

Well-meaning whites might include neoliberal white people who enjoy unearned benefits associated with whiteness and recognize shortcomings of the state, friends, and neighbors but do nothing meaningful to bring about change. They have relatively low race consciousness and low adherence to American civil religion. Well-meaning whites are complicit in the actions of white priestly preservationists because they do not actively work to confront them and the silence of many is equivalent to cosigning on their beliefs.

Race Consciousness

Low Race Consciousness	High Race Consciousness
White priestly preservationist Low race consciousness, high adherence in American civil religion, and advocates of race neutrality. White people fearful of perceived black progress demonstrate intense white religious shock and white fervor rooted in the victimization of white people, especially in contemporary times.	**Well-meaning whites** Low race consciousness, low adherence in American civil religion, and advocates of race neutrality. Neoliberal white people who enjoy unearned benefits associated with whiteness and recognize shortcomings of the state, friends, and neighbors but do nothing meaningful to challenge antiblack sentiments. Well-meaning whites are accomplices in the enduring racial divide.
Race contrarians High race consciousness, high adherence in American civil religion, and advocates of both racially neutral and race-conscious policies and practices. Racial and ethnic minorities who are relatively optimistic about the ability of America to reimagine and reinvent itself to become a more just and equitable society. May include recent immigrants influenced by the global myth of racism and individuals with low levels of linked racial fate or connection between what happens to black people affecting what happens to them.	**Race-transcendent prophets** High race consciousness, low adherence in American civil religion, and supports race-conscious initiatives. Black people engaged in passive and active forms of resistance to expose society as it is as opposed to society as it *ought* to be.

American Civil Religion

High Adherence to American Civil Religion	Low Adherence to American Civil Religion

Figure 1. Race Fairness, Race Consciousness, and the Belief in American Civil Religion Typology.

Race-transcendent prophets have high race consciousness and low adherence to American civil religion. Race-transcendent prophets include black people engaged in passive and active forms of resistance to expose society as it is as opposed to society as it ought to be. These individuals understand what Du Bois sought to capture in his discussion about the challenges associated with black people who must reconcile their racial identity and their "American" identity. Race-transcendent prophets are most at risk for physical and virtual effects on their bodies and their character. They understand the risks but are prepared to make the necessary sacrifices in the hope that change will come even if it is not during their lifetime.

Racial contrarians, on the other hand, have high race consciousness and high adherence to American civil religion. This type would likely include racial and ethnic minorities who are relatively optimistic about the ability of America to reimagine and reinvent itself to become a more just and equitable society. Racial contrarians may also include recent immigrants influenced by global myths about racism and antiblack sentiments. Much like the well-meaning whites, racial contrarians do little to bend the arc more toward justice by their unwillingness to be openly critical about the existing racial social order, while remaining susceptible to the white rage of disenchanted white workers, like the white priestly preservationists.

Only when public policies and private practices reflect an appreciation for the humanity and dignity of everyone, especially black people, who have endured some of the most horrific forms of injustices and atrocities in human history, will we begin to see a narrowing of the racial gaps between black people and white people on wealth, education, and in the criminal justice system. The alternative is more black deaths, more black bodies in physical bondage, and more black minds that never realize their full potential. The time has long since passed for America to get off the road it is on and find its way to a destination that lives up to its articulated commitment to fairness, equity, and justice for all.

References

Aja, Alan, Daniel Bustillo, William Darity, and Darrick Hamilton. 2014a. "From a Tangle of Pathology to a Race-Fair America." *Dissent* (Summer 2014): 39–43.

Aja, Alan, Daniel Bustillo, William Darity, and Darrick Hamilton. 2014b. "Jobs Instead of Austerity: A Bold Policy Proposal for Economic Justice." *Social Research* 80(3): 781–794.

Alesse, Liz. 2020. "With Constitutional Questions Murky, Some Churches Continue to Defy Restrictions on Gatherings." *ABC News*, April 5. https://abcnews. go.com/Health/constitutional-questions-murky-churches-continue-defy-restrictions-gatherings/story?id=69973339.

Allen, Greg, and Kelly McEvers. 2017. "Justice Department Declines to Prosecute Police Officers in Killing of Alton Sterling." *All Things Considered*, May 3. Transcript.

Alozie, Nicolas. 1995. "Political Tolerance Hypotheses and White Opposition to a Martin Luther King Holiday in Arizona." *Social Science Journal* 32(1): 1–16.

America, Richard. 2002. *The Wealth of Races*. Santa Barbara, CA: Praeger.

Anderson, Carol. 2016. *White Rage: The Unspoken Truth of Our Racial Divide*. New York: Bloomsbury, 2016.

Anderson, Elijah. 1990. *Streetwise: Race, Class, and Change in an Urban Community*. Chicago: University of Chicago Press.

Archer, Deborah. 2009. "Introduction: Challenging the School-to-Prison Pipeline." *New York Law School Review* 54(4): 867–872.

Armstrong, Elizabeth, and Laura Hamilton. 2015. *Paying for the Party: How College Maintains Inequality*. Cambridge, MA: Harvard University Press.

Arnett Ferguson, Ann. 2001. *Bad Boys: Public Schools in the Making of Black Masculinity*. Ann Arbor: University of Michigan Press.

Arnold, David, Will Dobbie, and Crystal Yang. 2017. "Racial Bias in Bail Decisions." *Quarterly Journal of Economics* 133(4): 1885–1932.

Associated Press. 2017. "Key Facts in the Shooting Death of Alton Sterling." *US News Online*, May 2. https://apnews.com/9e931627f5b84898a949ca51ca697e04/Key-facts-in-the-shooting-death-of-Alton-Sterling.

Attard, Jamie. 2012. "Life Bonds: Linking Returns of Life Outcomes." *Stanford Social Innovation Review*, September 12. https://ssir.org/articles/entry/life_bonds_linking_returns_to_life_outcomes.

Au, Wayne, and Joseph Ferrare. 2015. *Mapping Corporate Education Reform: Power and Policy Networks in the Neoliberal State*. New York: Routledge.

Baradaran, Mehrsa. 2019. *The Color of Money: Black Banks and the Racial Wealth Gap*. Cambridge, MA: Harvard University Press.

Barlow, Kathleen, and C. Elaine Dunbar. 2010. "Race, Class, and Whiteness in Gifted and Talented Identification: A Case Study." *Berkeley Review of Education* 1(1): 63–85.

Barlow, Michael. 2016. "Addressing Shortcomings in Afro-Pessimism." *Inquiries Journal* 8(9): 1–2.

Barnes, Mario. 2019. "We Will Turn Back? On Why *Regents of the University of California v. Bakke* Makes the Case for Adopting More Radically Race-Conscious Admissions Policies." *U.C. Davis Law Review* 52(5): 2265–2303.

Barrera, Mario. 1979. *Race and Class in the Southwest: A Theory of Racial Inequality*. Notre Dame, IN: Notre Dame University Press.

Beck, Brenden. 2019. "Broken Windows in the Cul-de-Sac? Race/Ethnicity and Quality-of-Life Policing in the Changing Suburbs." *Crime and Delinquency* 65(2): 270–292.

Bell, Derrick. 1970. *Race, Racism and American Law*. New York: Aspen.

Bell, Derrick. 1980. "*Brown v. Board of Education* and the Interest-Convergence Dilemma." *Harvard Law Review* 93(3): 518–533.

Bell, Derrick. 1992a. "Racial Realism." *Connecticut Law Review* 24(2): 363–379.

Bell, Derrick. 1992b. *Faces at the Bottom of the Well: The Permanence of Racism*. New York: Basic Books.

Bell, Jeannine. 2019. "The Hidden Fences Shaping Resegregation." *Harvard Civil Rights-Civil Liberties Law Review* 54(2): 813–828.

Bellah, Robert. 1967. "Civil Religion in America." *Daedalus: Journal of the American Academy of Arts and Sciences* 96(1): 1–21.

Belson, Ken. 2017. "Players Criticize N.F.L. Over Donation Proposal." *New York Times*, November 29. https://www.nytimes.com/2017/11/29/sports/football/nfl-players-coalition.html.

Berry, Mary Frances. "Vindicating Martin Luther King, Jr.: The Road to a Color-Blind Society." *Journal of Negro History* 81(1/4): 137–144.

"Beyond Suspensions: Examining School Discipline Policies and Connections to the School-to-Prison Pipeline for Students of Color with Disabilities." 2019. Washington, DC: U.S. Commission on Human Rights. https://www.usccr.gov/pubs/2019/07-23-Beyond-Suspensions.pdf.

Bigg, Matthew. 2018. "Election of Obama Provokes Rise in Hate Crimes." *Reuters*, November 24. https://www.reuters.com/article/us-usa-obama-hatecrimes-idUSTRE4AN81U20081124.

Bishop, Greg, and Ben Baskin. 2017. "The Kap Effect." *Sports Illustrated*, December 11. https://vault.si.com/vault/2017/12/11/kap-effect.

Blake, Charles. 2020. "Presiding Bishop's Update on COVID-19." Church of God in Christ, Memphis, Tennessee, March 25. https://www.cogic.org/covid19/presiding-bishops-covid-19-update-3-25-20/.

Blauner, Robert. 1972. *Racial Oppression in America*. New York: Harper & Row.

Bobo, Lawrence, and Vincent L. Hutchings. 1996. "Perceptions of Racial Group Competition: Extending Blumer's Theory of Group Position to a Multiracial Social Context." *American Sociological Review* 61: 951–972.

Boesler, Michael. 2019. "U.S. Can Shrink the Racial Wealth Gap with 'Baby Bonds.'" *Crains Cleveland*, May 18. https://www.crainscleveland.com/finance/us-can-shrink-racial-wealth-gap-baby-bonds.

Bonilla-Silva, Eduardo. 1997. "Rethinking Racism: Toward a Structural Interpretation." *American Sociological Review* 62(3): 465–480.

Bonilla-Silva, Eduardo. 2013. *Racism without Racists: Color-Blind Racism and the Persistence of Racial Inequality in the United States*. Lanham, MD: Rowman & Littlefield.

Botha, M. Elaine. 1983. "Black and White Civil Religion Ideology." *Bulletin for Christian Scholarship* 48(4): 249–258.

Bradley, Stefan. 2018. *Upending the Ivory Tower: Civil Rights, Black Power, and the Ivy League*. New York: New York University Press.

Braga, Anthony, Rod Brunson, and Kevin Drakulich. 2019. "Race, Place, and Effective Policing." *Annual Review of Sociology* 45(1): 535–555.

Brooks, Evelyn. 1988. "Religion, Politics, and Gender: The Leadership of Nannie Helen Burroughs." *Journal of Religious Thought* 44(2): 7–23.

Brown v. Board of Education, 347 U.S. 483 (1954).

Brown, Michael, Martin Carnoy, Elliot Currie, Troy Duster, David Oppenheimer, Marjorie Shultz, and David Wellman. 2003. *Whitewashing Race: The Myth of a Color-Blind Society*. Berkeley: University of California Press.

Bruenig, Matt. 2018. "Social Wealth Fund for America." *People's Policy Project*, July. https://www.peoplespolicyproject.org/wp-content/uploads/2018/07/Social WealthFund.pdf.

Bruenig, Matt. 2019. "Baby Bonds Only Modestly Reduce the Racial Wealth Gap." *People's Policy Project*, January 22. https://www.peoplespolicyproject.org/2019/01/22/baby-bonds-only-modestly-reduce-the-racial-wealth-gap/.

Brunsma, David, Eric Brown, and Peggy Placier. 2013. "Teaching Race at Historically White Colleges and Universities: Identifying and Dismantling the Walls of Whiteness." *Critical Sociology* 39(5): 717–738.

Buozis, Michael. 2018. "'Bizarre Dissonances in Baltimore': Class and Race in the Color-blind Discourses of Police Violence." *Democratic Communique* 27(2): 36–52.

Buras, Kristen. 2011. "Race, Charter Schools, and Conscious Capitalism." *Harvard Educational Review* 81(2): 296–331.

Burkett, Randall. 1978. *Garveyism as a Religious Movement: The Institutionalization of a Black Civil Religion.* New York: Oxford University Press.

Butler, Paul. 2017. *Chokehold.* New York: New Press.

Byrd, W. Carson. 2017. "Inflective and Reflective Whiteness in the Sociology of Race and Ethnicity. A Comment on an Integrative Framework for the Field." *Ethnicity and Racial Studies* 40(13): 2226–2231.

Cannon, Lou. 1977. "Bakke Also Vied with the Well-to-Do." *Washington Post,* October 2. https://www.washingtonpost.com/archive/politics/1977/10/02/bakke-also-vied-with-the-well-to-do/df551af7-c055-4053-8cb0-38099b81bcdc/.

Capper, Colleen. 2015. "The 20th Year Anniversary of Critical Race Theory in Education: Implications for Leading to Eliminate Racism." *Educational Administration Quarterly* 51(5): 791–833.

Carr, Paul. 2016. "Whiteness and White Privilege: Problematizing Race and Racism in a 'Color-Blind' World, and in Education." *International Journal of Critical Pedagogy* 7(1): 51–74.

Carson, Clayborne. 1998. *The Autobiography of Martin Luther King, Jr.* New York: Grand Central.

Chow, Rosalind, and Eric Knowles. 2015. "Taking Race Off the Table: Agenda Setting and Support for Colorblind Public Policy." *Personality and Social Psychology Bulletin* (October 19): 1–15.

Ciribassi, Rebekah, and Crystal Patil. 2016. "We Don't Wear It on Our Sleeve: Sickle Cell Disease and the (in)Visible Body in Parts." *Social Science and Medicine* 148: 131–138.

Clancy, Margaret, Sondra Beverly, Michael Sherraden, and Jin Huang. 2016. "Testing Universal Child Development Accounts: Financial Effects in a Large Social Experiment." *Social Science Review* 90(4): 683–708.

Cloud, Matthew. 2004. "One Nation, Under God: Tolerable Acknowledgment of Religion or Unconstitutional Cold War Propaganda Cloaked in American Civil Religion?" *Journal of Church and State* 46(2): 311–340.

Collins, Patricia Hill. 2000. *Black Feminist Thought.* New York: Routledge.

Cook-Martin, David, and David Scott FitzGerald. 2017. *Culling the Masses: The Democratic Origins of Racial Immigration Policy in America.* Cambridge, MA: Harvard University Press.

Coughlan, Ryan. 2018. "Divergent Trends in Neighborhood and School Segregation in the Age of School Choice." *Peabody Journal of Education* 93(4): 349–366.

Craemer, Thomas. 2018. "International Reparations for Slavery and the Slave Trade." *Journal of Black Studies* 49(7): 694–713.

Craven, Julia. 2016. "More than 250 Black People Were Killed by Police in 2016." *Politics,* July 7. https://www.huffpost.com/entry/black-people-killed-by-police-america_n_577da633e4b0c590f7e7fb17.

Craven, Julia. 2017. "32 Blue Lives Matter Bills Have Been Introduced Across 14 States This Year." *HuffPost,* March 1. https://www.huffpost.com/entry/blue-black-lives-matter-police-bills-states_n_58b61488e4b0780bac2e31b8.

Curry, Tommy. 2017. "Africana Philosophy: The Development of the Discipline in the United States." *Choice* 54(9): http://ala-choice.libguides.com/c.php?g=652506.

da Costa Pedro. 2019. "America's Humongous Wealth Gap Is Widening Further." *Forbes*, May 29. https://www.forbes.com/sites/pedrodacosta/2019/05/29/americas-humungous-wealth-gap-is-widening-further/#7e6aac0842ee.

Delgado, Daniel Justino. 2018. " 'My Deputies Arrest Anyone Who Breaks the Law': Understanding How Color-blind Discourse and Reasonable Suspicion Facilitate Racist Policing." *Sociology of Race and Ethnicity* 4(4): 541–554.

Dancy, T. Elon. 2014. "(Un)Doing Hegemony in Education: Disrupting School-to-Prison Pipelines for Black Males." *Equity and Excellence in Education* 47(4): 476–493.

Darby, Derrick, and Argun Saatcioglu. 2015. "Race, Inequality of Opportunity, and School Choice." *Theory and Research in Education* 13(1): 56–86.

Darity, William A. 2008. "Forty Acres and a Mule for the 21st Century." *Social Science Quarterly* 89: 656–664.

Darity, William A. 2019. "The Big Idea—Baby Bonds: A Leg Up for Everyone." https://sanford.duke.edu/articles/multimedia-feature-big-idea-baby-bonds.

Darity, William A., and Dania Frank. 2003. "The Political Economy of Ending Racism and the WCAR: The Economics of Reparations." *American Economic Review* 93(2): 326–329.

Darity, William A., Bidisha Lahiri, and Dania Frank. D. 2010. "Reparations for African Americans as a Transfer Problem: A Cautionary Tale." *Review of Development Economics* 14: 248–261.

Davis, Angela J., ed. 2017. *Policing the Black Man.* New York: Pantheon Books.

Davis, Tomeka. 2014. "School Choice and Segregation: Racial Equality in Magnet Schools." *Education and Urban Society* 46(4): 399–433.

De La Cruz-Viesca, Melany, Paul M. Ong, Andre Comandon, William Darity, and Darrick Hamilton. 2018. "Fifty Years After the Kerner Commission Report: Place, Housing, and Racial Wealth Inequality in Los Angeles." *Russell Sage Foundation Journal of the Social Sciences* 4(6): 160–184.

Delmont, Matthew. 2016. *Why Busing Failed: Race, Media, and the National Resistance to School Desegregation.* Oakland: University of California Press.

Delpit, Lisa. 2006. *Other People's Children: Cultural Conflict in the Classroom.* New York: York University Press.

Dias, Robette Ann. 2016. "Racism Creates Barriers to Effective Community Policing." *Southern Illinois University Law Journal* 40: 501–512.

Dixon, Adrienne D., and Celia K. Rousseau. 2006. *Critical Race Theory in Education Theory: All God's Children Got a Song.* New York: Routledge.

Douglas, Andrew. 2018. "Diagnosing Racial Capitalism." *Boston Review* (Winter): 40–44.

Douglass, Patrice, and Frank Wilderson. 2013. "The Violence of Presence: Metaphysics in a Blackened World." *Black Scholar* 43(4): 117–123.

Drakulich, Kevin, John Hagan, Devon Johnson, and Kevin H. Wozniak. 2017. "Race, Justice, Policing, and the 2016 American Presidential Election." *Du Bois Review: Social Science Research on Race* 14(1): 7–33.

Du Bois, W. E. B. 1903. *Souls of Black Folk*. Chicago: McClurg & Co.

Du Bois, W.E.B. [1903] 1993. *Souls of Black Folk*. New York: Knopf.

Du Bois, W. E. B. [1921] 1975. *Darkwater: Voices from Within the Veil*. New York: Harcourt, Brace.

Du Bois, W.E.B. [1935] 1962. *Black Reconstruction in America*. New York: Free Press.

Du Bois, W. E. B. 1995. *The Philadelphia Negro*. Philadelphia: University of Pennsylvania Press.

Duncan, Garrett Albert. 2005. "Black Youth, Identity, and Ethics." *Educational Theory* 55(1): 3–22.

Duncan, Greg, and Richard Murnane. 2014. *Restoring Opportunity: The Crisis of Inequality and the Challenge for American Education*. Cambridge, MA: Harvard Educational.

Editors of *GQ*. 2017. "Colin Kaepernick Is GQ's Citizen of the Year." *GQ*, November 13. https://www.gq.com/story/colin-kaepernick-cover-men-of-the-year.

Elliott, William, Kevin Kim, Hyunzee Jung, and Min Zhan. 2010. "Asset Holding and Educational Attainment among African American Youth." *Children and Youth Services Review* 32(11): 1497–1507.

Erzen, Tanya. 2001. "Turnstile Jumpers and Broken Windows: Policing Disorder in New York City." In *Zero Tolerance: Quality of Life and the New Police Brutality in New York City*, edited by A. McArdle and T. Erzen, 19–49. New York: New York University Press.

Evans, Matthew, and David Wilkins. 2019. "Transformative Justice, Reparations and Transatlantic Slavery." *Social and Legal Studies* 28(2): 137–157.

Fader, Jamie, Megan Kurlchek, and Kirstin Morgan. 2014. "The Color of Juvenile Justice: Racial Disparities in Dispositional Decisions." *Social Science Research* 44: 126–140.

Fasching-Varner, Kenneth, Lori Latrice Martin, Roland Mitchell, and Karen Bennett-Haron. 2014. "Beyond School-to-Prison Pipeline and Toward an Educational and Penal Realism." *Equity and Excellence in Education* 47(4): 410–429.

Fasching-Varner, Kenneth, Lori Latrice Martin, Roland Mitchell, Karen Bennett-Haron, and Arash Daneshzadeh. 2017. *Understanding, Dismantling, and Disrupting the Prison-to-School Pipeline*. Lanham, MD: Lexington Books.

Feagin, Joe, and Clairece Booher Feagin. 1978. "Institutionalized Discrimination." In *Discrimination American Style: Institutional Racism and Sexism*, edited by J. Feagin and C. Feagin, 19–41. Malabar, FL: Robert E. Krieger.

Feldman, Guy. 2018. "Saving from Poverty: A Critical Review of Individual Development Accounts." *Critical Social Policy* 38(2): 181–200.

Ferguson, Ann A. 2001. *Bad Boys: Public Schools in the Making of Black Masculinity*. Ann Arbor: University of Michigan Press.

Fernandez, Roberto M., and Isabel Fernandez-Mateo. 2006. "Networks, Race, and Hiring." *American Sociological Review* 71(1): 42–71.

Fine, Michelle. 1991. *Framing Dropouts: Notes on the Politics of an Urban High School.* Albany: State University of New York Press.

Finley, Stephen C., Biko Mandela Gray, and Lori Latrice Martin, eds. 2020. *The Religion of White Rage.* Edinburgh: Edinburgh University Press.

Finley, Stephen C., Biko Mandela Gray, and Lori Latrice Martin. 2018. "Affirming Our Values." *Journal of Academic Freedom* 9: 1–20.

Finley, Stephen C., and Lori Latrice Martin. 2017. "The Complexity of Color and the Religion of Whiteness." In *Color Struck*, edited by L. L. Martin, H. D. Horton, C. Herring, C. V. Keith, and M. Thomas, 179–196. Leiden: Senses/Brill.

Flynn, Andrea, Susan Holmber, Dorian Warren, and Felicia Wong. 2016. "Rewrite the Racial Rules: Building an Inclusive American Economy." *Roosevelt Institute*, June 2016. https://rooseveltinstitute.org/wp-content/uploads/2016/06/Structural-Discrimination-Final.pdf.

Fordham, Signithia. 1988. "Racelessness as a Factor in Black Students' School Success: Pragmatic Strategy or Pyrrhic Victory?" *Harvard Educational Review* 58(1): 54–85.

Forlitit, Amy. 2017. "The Police Officer Who Shot Philando Castile Will Be Paid $48,500 in a Buyout." *USA Today*, July 10. https://www.usatoday.com/story/news/nation/2017/07/11/cop-who-killed-philando-castile-paid-48-500-buyout/466918001/.

Forman, James. 2017. *Locking Up Our Own.* New York: Farrar, Straus and Giroux.

Frank, David. 2011. "Obama's Rhetorical Signature: Cosmopolitan Civil Religion in the Presidential Inaugural Address, January 20, 2009." *Rhetoric and Public Affairs* 14: 605–630.

Frankenberg, Erica, Genevieve Siegel-Hawley, and Jia Wang. 2010. "Choice without Equity: Charter School Segregation and the Need for Civil Rights Standards." https://epaa.asu.edu/ojs/article/view/779.

Frazier, E. Franklin. 1937. "Negro Harlem: An Ecological Study." *American Journal of Sociology* 43(1): 72–88.

Frazier, E. Franklin. 1939. *The Negro Family in the United States.* Chicago: University of Chicago Press.

Frazier, E. Franklin. 1957. *Black Bourgeoisie.* New York: Free Press.

Frazier, E. Franklin. 1974. *The Negro Church in America.* Sourcebooks in Negro History.

Frazier, E. Franklin. 1927. "The Pathology of Racial Prejudice." *Forum* 70: 856–862.

Freidus, Alexandra. 2019. "A Great School Benefits Us All": Advantaged Parents and the Gentrification of an Urban Public School." *Urban Education* 54(8): 1121–1148.

Fryer, Roland. 2016. "An Empirical Analysis of Racial Differences in Police Use of Force." NBER Working Paper Series, Working Paper 22399.

Gans, Herbert. 1979. "Symbolic Ethnicity: The Future of Ethnic Groups and Cultures in America." *Ethnic and Racial Studies* 2: 1–20.

Gomez-Velez, Natalie. 2015. "Can Universal Pre-K Overcome Extreme Race and Income Segregation to Reach New York's Neediest Children? The Importance of Legal Infrastructure and the Limits of the Law." *Cleveland State Law Review* 63(2): 319–354.

Goodman, Peter. 2008. "Too Big to Fail?" *New York Times*, July 7. https://www.nytimes.com/2008/07/20/weekinreview/20goodman.html.

Gould, Mark. 1999. "Race and Theory: Culture, Poverty, and Adaptation to Discrimination in Wilson and Ogbu." *Sociological Theory* 17: 171–200.

Gray, Biko M., and Stephen C. Finley. 2015. "God Is a White Racist: Immanent Atheism as a Religious Response to Black Lives Matter and Antiblack State-Sanctioned Violence." Published as part of a roundtable discussion in the *Journal of Africana Religions* 3(4): 443–453.

Gray, Biko Mandela, Stephen Finley, and Lori Latrice Martin. 2019. "High-Tech Lynching: White Virtual Mobs and University Administrators as Policing Agents in Higher Education." *Issues in Race and Society* 8: 147–176.

Grinstein-Weiss, Michael, Kate Irish, Susan Parish, and Kristen Wagner. 2007. "Using Individual Development Accounts to Save for a Home: Are There Differences by Race?" *Social Science Review* 81(4): 657–681.

Gupta-Kagan, Josh. 2019. "Reevaluating School Searches Following School-to-Prison Pipeline Reforms." *Fordham Law Review* 87(5): 1–46.

Hamilton, Darrick, and William Darity. 2010. "Can Baby Bonds Eliminate the Racial Wealth Gap in Putative Post-Racial America?" *Review of Black Political Economy* 37: 207–216.

Hammond, Phillip E. 1976. "The Sociology of American Civil Religion: A Bibliographical Essay." *Sociological Analysis* 37(2): 169–182.

Hammond, Phillip E., Amanda Porterfield, James G. Moseley, and Jonathan D. Sarna. 1994. "Forum: American Civil Religion Revisited." *Religion and American Culture: A Journal of Interpretation* 4(1): 1–23.

Hammonds, Evelynn, and Susan M. Reverby. 2019. "Toward a Historically Informed Analysis of Racial Health Disparities since 1619." *American Journal of Public Health* 109(10): 1348–1349.

Haney López, Ian F. 2000. "Institutional Racism: Judicial Conduct and a New Theory of Racial Discrimination." *Yale Law Journal* 109(8): 1717–1884.

Hankins, Katherine. 2007. "The Final Frontier: Charter Schools as New Community Institutions of Gentrification." *Urban Geography* 28(2): 113–128.

Harlan, John Marshall. "Dissent from Plessy v. Ferguson." 1896. Retrieved from http://wwphs.sharpschool.com/UserFiles/Servers/Server_10640642/File/bugge/Chapter%2017/washingtonvsdubois.PDF.

Harris, Angelique, David Nelson, Kimberly Salas Harris, Barbara Horner-Ibler, and Edith Burns. 2015. " 'We Need a New Normal': Sociocultural Constructions of Obesity and Overweight among African American Women." In *Black*

Sociology: Contemporary Issues and Future Directions, edited by E. Wright and E. Wallace, 177–179. Burlington, VT: Ashgate.

Harris, Frederick. 1999. *Something Within: Religion in African American Activism*. New York: Oxford University Press.

Hartman, Saidiya. 1997. *Scenes of Subjection: Terror, Slavery, and Self-Making in Nineteenth-Century America*. New York: Oxford University Press.

Hartman, Saidiya, and Frank Wilderson. 2003. "The Position of the Unthought." *Qui Parle* 13(2): 183–201.

Hauper, Shaun. 2009. "Niggers No More: A Critical Race Counternarrative on Black Male Achievement at Predominately White Colleges and Universities." *International Journal of Qualitative Studies in Education* (November–December): 697–712.

Haveman, Robert, and Edward Wolff. 2004. "The Concept and Measurement of Asset Poverty: Level, Trends and Composition for the U.S., 1983–2001." *Journal of Economic Inequality* 2: 145–169.

Heifetz, Ronald, Alexander Grashow, and Marty Linsky. 2009. *The Practice of Adaptive Leadership: Tools and Tactics for Changing Your Organization and the World*. Cambridge, MA: Harvard Business Press, 2009.

Heifetz, Ronald, and Marty Linsky. 2002. "A Survival Guide for Leaders." *Harvard Business Review* (June): https://hbr.org/2002/06/a-survival-guide-for-leaders.

Herbert, Christopher, and Winnie Tsen. 2005. "The Potential of Down-Payment Assistance for Increasing Homeownership among Minority and Low-Income Households." https://www.huduser.gov/publications/pdf/potentialdown paymentassistance.pdf.

Herring, Cedric, and Loren Henderson. 2016. "Wealth Inequality in Black and White." *Social Problems* 8: 4–17.

Hetey, Rebecca C., and Jennifer L. Eberhardt. 2018. "The Numbers Don't Speak for Themselves: Racial Disparities and the Persistence of Inequality in the Criminal Justice System." *Current Directions in Psychological Science* 27(3): 183–187.

Higginbotham, Evelyn Brooks. 1992. "African-American Women's History and the Metalanguage of Race." *Signs* 17(2): 251–274.

Hilbert, Jim. 2017. "Restoring the Promise of Brown: Using State Constitutional Law to Challenge School Segregation." *Journal of Law and Education* 46(1): 1–57.

Hinton, Elizabeth, LeShae Henderson, and Cindy Reed. 2018. "An Unjust Burden: The Disparate Treatment of Black Americans in the Criminal Justice System." Vera Institute of Justice. https://www.vera.org/publications/for-the-record-unjust-burden.

A History of the United States Saving Bonds Program. 1991. U.S. Savings Bonds Division. Department of Treasury. Washington, DC. https://www.treasury direct.gov/indiv/research/history/history_sb.pdf.

Holland, Joshua. 2016. "The Average Black Family Would Need 228 Years to Build the Wealth of a White Family Today." *Nation*, August 8. https://www.the

nation.com/article/archive/the-average-black-family-would-need-228-years-to-build-the-wealth-of-a-white-family-today/.

hooks, bell. 1988. *Teaching to Transgress: Education as the Practice of Freedom.* New York: Routledge.

Hope, John. 1896. "We Are Struggling for Equality." https://www.blackpast.org/african-american-history/1896-john-hope-we-are-struggling-equality/.

House Resolution 194. In the House of Representatives, U.S. July 29, 2008. https://www.congress.gov/110/bills/hres194/BILLS-110hres194eh.pdf.

Huang, Jin, Margaret Lombe, Michelle Putnam, Michal Grinstein-Weiss, and Michael Sherraden. 2016. "Individual Development Accounts and Home-ownership among Low-Income Adults with Disabilities: Evidence from a Randomized Experiment." *Journal of Applied Social Science* 10(1): 55–66.

Hucks, Tracey. 2012. *Yoruba Traditions and African American Religious Nationalism.* Albuquerque: University of New Mexico Press.

Hunt, Joel. 2019. "From Crime Mapping to Crime Forecasting: The Evolution of Place-Based Policing." National Institute of Justice. https://nij.ojp.gov/topics/articles/crime-mapping-crime-forecasting-evolution-place-based-policing.

Inequality.org. "Wealth inequality in America." https://inequality.org/facts/wealth-inequality/#household-wealth.

Intravia, Jonathan, Alex Piquero, and Nicole Leeper Piquero. 2017. "The Racial Divide Surrounding United States of America National Anthem Protests in the National Football League." *Deviant Behavior* 39: 1–11.

Jacobs, Nicholas. 2013. "Understanding School Choice: Location as a Determinant of Charter School Racial, Economic, and Linguistic Segregation." *Education and Urban Society* 45(4): 459–482.

Jones, Janelle. 2017. "The Racial Wealth Gap: How African Americans Have Been Short-Changed Out of Materials to Build Wealth." https://www.epi.org/blog/the-racial-wealth-gap-how-african-americans-have-been-shortchanged-out-of-the-materials-to-build-wealth/.

Jones, Sosanya Marie. 2014. "Diversity Leadership under Race-Neutral Policies in Higher Education." *Equality, Diversity and Inclusion* 33(8): 708–720.

Jordan, Caine, Guy Mount, and Kai Perry Parker. 2018. "A Disgrace to All Slave-Holders: The University of Chicago's Founding Ties to Slavery and the Path to Reparations." *Journal of African American History* 103(1–2): 163–178.

Joy, Meghan, and John Shields. 2013. "Social Impact Bonds: The Next Phase of Third Sector Marginalization." *Canadian Journal of Nonprofit and Social Economy Research* 4: 39–55.

Kamalu, Ngozi Caleb, Margery Coulson-Clark, and Nkechi Margaret Kamalu. 2010. "Racial Disparities in Sentencing: Implications for the Criminal Justice System and the African American Community." *African Journal of Criminology and Justice Studies* 4(1): 1–33.

Kao, Grace, and Jerome Copulsky. 2007. "The Pledge of Allegiance and the Meaning and Limits of Civil Religion." *Journal of the American Academy of Religion* 75(1): 121–149.

Karnowski, Steve. 2017. "Minnesota Police Officer Never Saw Philando Castile's Gun during Traffic Stop, Prosecutors Say." *Chicago Tribune*, June 12. https://www.chicagotribune.com/nation-world/ct-philando-castile-officer-trial-20170612-story.html.

Karpinski, Carol F. 2006. "Bearing the Burden of Desegregation: Black Principals and Brown." *Urban Education* 41(3): 237–276.

Kaufman, Emily 2016. "Policing Mobilities Through Bio-Spatial Profiling in New York City." *Political Geography* 55(1): 72–81.

Kaufman, Scott. 2013. *Ungifted: Intelligence Redefined*. New York: Basic Books.

Kayoko Peralta, Adriane. 2016. "A Market Analysis of Race-Conscious University Admissions for Students of Color." *Denver Law Review* 93(1): 173–217.

Keister, Lisa. 2000. *Wealth Inequality in America*. Cambridge, MA: Harvard University Press.

Kendi, Ibram. 2019. *How to Be an Antiracist*. New York: Penguin Random House.

Kertscher, Tom. 2017. "Pro-Sheriff David Clarke Group Says Clarke Called Black Lives Matter Hate Group, Terrorist Movement." *PolitiFact Wisconsin*, April 17. http://www.politifact.com/wisconsin/statements/2017/apr/17/sheriff-david-clarke-us-senate/pro-sheriff-david-clarke-group-says-clarke-called-/.

King, Katrina Quisumbing. 2019. "Recentering U.S. Empire: A Structural Perspective of the Colorline." *Sociology of Race and Ethnicity* 5: 11–25.

King, Martin Luther. 1963. "Letter from the Birmingham Jail." https://www.africa.upenn.edu/Articles_Gen/Letter_Birmingham.html.

King, Martin Luther. 1967. *Where Do We Go from Here: Chaos or Community?* Boston, MA: Beacon Press.

Kish, Zenia, and Justin Leroy. 2015. "Bonded Life: Technologies of Racial Finance from Slave Insurance to Philanthrocapital." *Cultural Studies* 29(5–6): 630–651.

Kochihar, Rakesh, and Anthony Cilluffo. 2017. "How Wealth Inequality Has Changed in the U.S. since the Great Recession by Race, Ethnicity and Income." *Pew Research Center*, November 1. https://www.pewresearch.org/fact-tank/2017/11/01/how-wealth-inequality-has-changed-in-the-u-s-since-the-great-recession-by-race-ethnicity-and-income/.

Kokaliari, Effrosyni, Ann W. Roy, and Joyce Taylor. 2019. "American Perspectives on Racial Disparities in Child Removals." *Child and Neglect* 90: 139–148.

Kozol, Jonathan. 1991. *Savage Inequalities: Children in America's Schools*. New York: Broadway Books.

Kozol, Jonathan. 2005. *The Shame of the Nation: The Restoration of Apartheid Schooling in America*. New York: Random House.

Kozol, Jonathan. 2008. "Our Educational Apartheid." *Race, Poverty and Environment* 15(2): 67–69.

Kozol, Jonathan. 2019. "Biden and Segregation." *Nation* 308(18): 1–3.

Labaree, David. 2010. *Someone Has to Fail: The Zero-Sum Game of Public Schooling.* Cambridge, MA: Harvard University Press.

Lanard, Noah. 2019. "Louisiana Decided to Curb Mass Incarceration, Then ICE Showed Up." *Mother Jones*, May 1. https://www.motherjones.com/politics/2019/05/louisiana-decided-to-curb-mass-incarceration-then-ice-showed-up/.

Lawrence, Matthew. 1987. "The Id, the Ego, and Equal Protection: Reckoning with Unconscious Racism." *Stanford Law Review* 39: 317–388.

Lawrence, Matthew. 2008. "Symposium: Unconscious Discrimination Twenty-Years Later: Application and Evolution: Keynote Speakers: Unconscious Racism Revisited: Reflections on the Impact and Origins of the Id, the Ego, and Equal Protection." *Connecticut Law Review* 40: 1–34.

Leonardo, Zeus. 2013. "The Story of Schooling: Critical Race Theory and the Educational Racial Contract." *Discourse: Studies in the Cultural Politics of Education* 34(4): 599–610.

Leong, Nancy. 2013. "Racial Capitalism." *Harvard Law Review* 26: 2151–2226.

Levy, Tal. 2010. "Charter Schools Legislation and the Element of Race." *Western Journal of Black Studies* 34(1): 43–52.

Lewis, Amanda. 2003. *Race in the Schoolyard: Negotiating the Color Line in Classrooms and Communities.* New Brunswick, NJ: Rutgers University Press.

Lewis, Danny. 2016. "Five Times the United States Officially Apologized." *Smithsonian Magazine*, May 27. https://www.smithsonianmag.com/smart-news/five-times-united-states-officially-apologized-180959254/.

Lewis, Oscar. 1966. "The Culture of Poverty." *Scientific American* 215(4):19–25.

Levine, Murray, and Adeline Gordon Levine. 2012. "Education Deformed: No Child Left Behind and the Race to the Top. 'This Almost Reads Like Our Business Plan.'" *American Journal of Orthopyschiatry* 82(1): 104–113.

Li, Bethany. 2016. "Now Is the Time! Challenging Resegregation and Displacement in the Age of Hypergentrification." *Fordham Law Review* 85(3): 1189–1242.

Liberson, Stanley. 1980. *A Piece of the Pie: Black and White Immigrants since 1880.* Berkeley: University of California Press.

Lienesch, Michael. 2018. "Contesting Civil Religion: Religious Responses to American Patriotic Nationalism, 1919–1929." *Religion and American Culture* 28(1): 92–134.

Lipsitz, George. 2011. *How Racism Takes Place.* Philadelphia: Temple University Press.

Logan, John, and Julia Burkick-Will. 2017. "School Segregation and Disparities in Urban, Suburban, and Rural Areas." *Annals of the American Academy of Political and Social Science* 674(1): 199–216.

Lombardo, Robert, and Todd Lough. 2007. "Community Policing: Broken Windows, Community Building, and Satisfaction with the Police." *Police Journal* 80: 117–140.

Long, Charles. 1999. *Significations*. Aurora, CO: Davies Group.

Long, Heather. 2020. "U.S. Now Has 22 Million Unemployed, Wiping Out a Decade of Job Gains." *Washington Post*, April 16. https://www.washingtonpost.com/business/2020/04/16/unemployment-claims-coronavirus/.

"Louisiana's 2017 Criminal Justice Reform." 2018. *The PEW Charitable Trusts*, March 1. https://www.pewtrusts.org/en/research-and-analysis/issue-briefs/2018/03/louisianas-2017-criminal-justice-reforms.

Loury, Glenn C. 2008. *Race, Incarceration, and American Values*. Cambridge, MA: MIT Press.

Lyons, Christopher J., and Becky Pettit. 2011. "Compounded Disadvantage: Race, Incarceration, and Wage Growth." *Social Problems* 58: 257–280.

Maier, Florentine, Gian Barbetta, and Franka Godina. 2018. "Paradoxes of Social Impact Bonds." *Social Policy and Administration* 52(7): 1332–1353.

Marable, Manning. 2007. *Race, Reform, and Rebellion*. Jackson: University Press of Mississippi.

Markoff, S., R. Loya, and J, Santos. 2018. "Quick Guide to CSA Research: An Overview of Evidence on Children's Savings Accounts." https://prosperitynow.org/resources/quick-guide-csa-research-overview-evidence-childrens-savings-accounts.

Marks, E., G. Engelhardt, B. Rhodes, I. Wallace. 2014. "SEED for Oklahoma Kids: The Impact Evaluation. https://www.rti.org/sites/default/files/resources/seed_ok_impact_eval_rpt.pdf.

Martin, John, James Murphy, and Rick Moore. 2018. "Protest Movements and Citizen Discontent: Occupy Wall Street and the Tea Party." *Sociological Forum* 33: 575–595.

Martin, Lori Latrice. 2013. *Black Asset Poverty and the Enduring Racial Divide*. Boulder, CO: First Forum Press.

Martin, Lori Latrice. 2015. *Big Box Schools: Race, Education and the Danger of the Wal-Martization of Public Schools in America*. Lanham, MD: Lexington Books.

Martin, Lori Latrice. 2017. *White Sports Black Sports*. Santa Barbara, CA: Praeger.

Martin, Lori Latrice. 2018. "The Politics of Sports and Protest: Colin Kaepernick and the Practice of Leadership." *American Studies Journal* 64: DOI 10.18422/64-06.

Martin, Lori Latrice. 2019. "Race, Wealth, and Homesteading Revisited: How Public Policies Destroy(ed) Black Wealth." In *How Public Policy Impacts Racial Inequality*, edited by J. Grimm and J. Loke, 140–165. Baton Rouge: Louisiana State University Press.

Martin, Lori Latrice, and Raymond Jetson. 2017. *South Baton Rouge*. Charleston: Arcadia.

Martin, Steve, and George McHendry. 2016. "Kaepernick's Stand: Patriotism, Protest, and Professional Sports." *Journal of Contemporary Rhetoric* 6(3–4): 88–98.

Massey, Douglas S., and Nancy A. Denton. 1993. *American Apartheid: Segregation and the Making of the Underclass.* Cambridge, MA: Harvard University Press.

Mazzei, Patricia. 2020. "Florida Pastor Arrested after Defying Virus Orders." *New York Times*, March 30. https://www.nytimes.com/2020/03/30/us/coronavirus-pastor-arrested-tampa-florida.html.

McDermott, Monica. 2006. *Working-Class White: The Making and Unmaking of Race Relations.* Berkeley: University of California Press.

Melamed, Jodi. 2015. "Racial Capitalism." *Critical Ethnic Studies* 1(1): 76–85.

Meyerson, Collier. 2017. "The Case against 'Blue Lives Matter' Bills." *Nation*, May 23. https://www.thenation.com/article/archive/case-blue-lives-matter-bills/.

Michigan Freedom Fund. https://www.michiganfreedomfund.com/our-mission.

Miller, Melinda C. 2011. "Land and Racial Wealth Inequality." *American Economic Review* 101(3): 371–376.

Morgan, Jennifer L. 2015. "Archives and Histories of Racial Capitalism." *Social Text* 33 4(125): 153–161.

Morrier, Michael, and Peggy Gallagher. 2012. "Racial Disparities in Preschool Special Education Eligibility for Five Southern States." *Journal of Special Education* 46(3): 152–169.

Morris, Monique W. 2016. *Pushout: The Criminalization of Black Girls in Schools.* New York: New Press.

Moynihan, Daniel Patrick. 1965. *The Negro Family: The Case for National Action.* Washington, DC: Office of Planning and Research.

Mutchler, Jan, Yang Li, and Ping Xu. 2016. "Living Below the Line: Economic Insecurity and Older Americans' Insecurity in the States 2016." Center for Social and Demographic Research on Aging Publications. Paper 13. http://scholarworks.umb.edu/demographyofaging/13.

National Commission on Excellence. 1983. *A Nation at Risk: The Imperative for Educational Reform.* Washington, DC: United States Department of Education.

National Institute of Justice. 2017. Policing Research Plan: 2017–2022.

Neyland, Daniel. 2018. "On the Transformation of Children At-Risk into an Investment Proposition: A Study of Social Impact Bonds as an Anti-Market Devise." *Sociological Review* 66(3): 492–510.

Norris v. Alabama, 294 U.S. 587 (1935).

Nuno, Luis. 2013. "Police, Public Safety, and Race-Neutral Discourse." *Social Compass* 7(6): 471–486.

Oberman, Jonathan, and Kendea Johnson. 2016. "The Never Ending Tale: Racism and Inequality in the Era of Broken Windows." *Cardoza Law Review* 37: 1075–1091.

Oliver, Melvin L., and Thomas M. Shapiro. 1995. *Black Wealth / White Wealth: A New Perspective on Racial Inequality.* New York: Routledge.

Oliver, Melvin, and Thomas Shapiro. 2019. "Disrupting the Racial Wealth Gap." *Contexts* 18: 16–21.

Omi, Michael, and Howard Winant. 1994. *Racial Formation in the United States: From the 1960s to the 1990s.* 2nd ed. New York: Routledge & Kegan Paul.

Onwuachi-Willig, Angela. 2018. "From *Loving v. Virginia* to *Washington v. Davis*: The Erosion of the Supreme Court's Equal Protection Intent Analysis." *Virginia Journal of Social Policy and Law* 303: 304–316.

Onwuachi-Willig, Angela. 2019. "Reconceptualizing the Harms of Discrimination: How *Brown v. Board of Education* Helped to Further White Supremacy." *Virginia Law Review* 105(2): 343–369.

Pager, Devah, and Lincoln Quillian. 2005. "What Employers Say versus What They Do." *American Sociological Review* 70: 355–380.

Papenfuss, Mary. 2020. "COVID-19 Protestors Just Like Rosa Parks." *Daily Mail.com*, April 18. https://www.dailymail.co.uk/news/article-8227325/Lawyer-evangelical-megachurch-defying-social-distancing-orders-hospital-coronavirus.html.

Pattillo, Mary. 2005. "Black Middle-Class Neighborhoods." *Annual Review of Sociology* 35: 305–329.

Perkinson, James. 2004. *White Theology: Outing Supremacy in Modernity.* New York: Palgrave Macmillan.

Perry, Andre, David Harsbarger, and Carl Romer. 2020. "Mapping Racial Inequity amid COVID-19 Underscores Policy Discriminations against Black Americans." *Brookings*, April 16. https://www.brookings.edu/blog/the-avenue/2020/04/16/mapping-racial-inequity-amid-the-spread-of-covid-19/.

Pinder, Kamina Aliya. 2013. "Reconciling Race-Neutral Strategies and Race-Conscious Objectives: The Potential Resurgence of the Structural Injunction in Education Litigation." *Stanford Journal of Civil Rights and Civil Liberties* 9(2): 247–279.

"Policing the Black Man: A Conversation with Angela Davis and Sherrilyn Ifill." 2017. *Open Society Foundation*, September 6. https://www.opensociety foundations.org/events/policing-black-man-conversation-angela-j-davis-and-sherrilyn-ifill.

"Policing: Strategic Research Plan: 2017–2022." 2017. Washington, DC: National Institute of Justice.

Pollock, Mica. 2014. *Colormute: Race Talk Dilemmas in an American School.* Princeton, NJ: Princeton University Press.

Powell, Cedric, and Laura McNeal. 2018. "Dismantling Structural Inequality: Lock Ups, Systemic Chokeholds, and Race-Based Policing—A Symposium Summary." *University of Louisville Law Review* 57(1): 1–5.

Prasad, Monica. 2014. *The Land of Too Much: American Abundance and the Paradox of Poverty.* Cambridge, MA: Harvard University Press.

Putnam, Robert. 2015. *Our Kids: The American Dream in Crisis.* New York: Simon & Schuster.

R. L. 2013. "Wanderings of the Slave: Black Life and Social Death." *Mute*, June 5. https://www.metamute.org/editorial/articles/wanderings-slave-black-life-and-social-death.

Rabaka, Reiland. 2007. "The Souls of White Folk: W. E. B. Du Bois's Critique of White Supremacy and Contributions to Critical White Studies." *Journal of African American Studies* 11(1): 1–15.

Rahl, Kylie. 2016. "Racing to Neutrality: How Race-Neutral Admissions Programs Threaten the Future Use of Race-Based Affirmative Action in Higher Education." *Texas Tech Law Review* 49(1): 109–147.

Ray, Rashawn. 2020. "Why Are Blacks Dying at Higher Rates from COVID-19?" *Brookings*, April 9. https://www.brookings.edu/blog/fixgov/2020/04/09/why-are-blacks-dying-at-higher-rates-from-covid-19/.

Ray, Victor Erik, Antonia Randolph, Megan Underhill, and David Luke. 2017. "Critical Race Theory, Afro-Pessimism, and Racial Progress Narratives." *Sociology of Race and Ethnicity* 3(2): 1–12.

"Report of the Sentencing Project to the United Nations Special Rapporteur on Contemporary Forms of Racism, Racial Discrimination, Xenophobia, and Related Intolerance: Regarding Racial Disparities in the United States Criminal Justice System." 2018. Washington, DC: The Sentencing Project. Research and Advocacy for Reform.

"Report on the National Advisory Commission on Civil Disorders Summary Report." 1968. http://www.eisenhowerfoundation.org/docs/kerner.pdf.

Rice, Stephen K., and Michael D. White. 2010. *Race, Ethnicity, and Policing: New and Essential Readings*. New York: New York University Press.

Rios, Victor. 2006. "The Hyper-Criminalization of Black and Latino Male Youth in the Era of Mass Incarceration." *Souls* 8(2): 40–54.

Roberts, Dorothy. 2011. *Fatal Invention: How Science, Politics, and Big Business Re-create Race in the Twenty-first Century*. New York: New Press.

Robinson, Cedric. 1983. *Black Marxism*. Chapel Hill: University of North Carolina Press.

Roediger, David R. 1999. *The Wages of Whiteness: Race and the Making of the American Working Class*. New York: Verso.

Rojas, Rick. 2019. "Suburbanites in Louisiana Vote to Create a New City of Their Own." *New York Times*, October 13. https://www.nytimes.com/2019/10/13/us/baton-rouge-st-george.html.

Roman, John, Kelly Walsh, Sam Bieler, and Samuel Taxy. 2015. "Pay for Success and Social Impact Bonds." *Urban Institute*, https://www.urban.org/sites/default/files/alfresco/publication-pdfs/413150-Pay-for-Success-and-Social-Impact-Bonds-Funding-the-Infrastructure-for-Evidence-Based.PDF.

Rooks, Noliwe. 2006. *White Money, Black Power: The Surprising History of African American Studies and the Crisis of Race in Higher Education*. Boston, MA: Beacon Press.

Saez, Emmanuel, and Gabriel Zucman. 2018. "Wealth Inequality in the United States since 1913: Evidence from Capitalized Income Tax Data." *Quarterly Journal of Economics* 131(2): 519–578.

Scott, Kendra, Ma Debbin, Melody Sadler, and Joshua Correll. 2017. "A Social Scientific Approach toward Understanding Racial Disparities in Police Shooting: Data from the Department of Justice (1980–2000)." *Journal of Social Issues* 73(4): 701–722.

Sexton, Jared. 2011. "The Social Life of Social Death: On Afro-Pessimism and Black Optimism." *In Tensions* 1–47.

Sexton, Jared. 2016. "Afro-Pessimism: The Unclear Word." *Rhizomes: Cultural Studies in Emerging Knowledge* 29: 1–21.

Sexton, Jared. 2017. "All Black Everything." *e-flux* 79. http://www.e-flux.com/journal/79/94158/all-black-everything/.

Shanks, Trina. 2014. "The Promise of Child Development Accounts." *Community Investments* 26: 12–15.

Sherraden, Michael, Margaret Clancy, Yunju Nam, Jin Huang, Youngmi Kim, Sondra Beverly, Lisa Reyes Mason, Trina R. Williams Shanks, Nora Ellen Wikoff, Mark Schreiner, and Jason Q. Purnell. 2018. "Universal and Progressive Child Development Accounts: A Policy Innovation to Reduce Educational Disparity." *Urban Education* 53(6): 806–833.

Soffer, Michael, Katherine McDonald, and Peter Blanck. 2010. "Poverty among Adults with Disabilities: Barriers to Promoting Asset Accumulation in Individual Development Accounts." *American Journal of Community Psychology* 46(3): 376–385.

Sommerfeldt, Chris. 2016. "Baton Rouge Settles Lawsuit Brought by Alton Sterling Protesters." *New York Daily News*, November 23. https://www.nydailynews.com/news/national/baton-rouge-settles-lawsuit-brought-alton-sterling-protesters-article-1.2884260.

Somvichian-Clausen, Austa. 2020. "Trump's Use of the Term 'Chinese Virus' for Coronavirus Hurts Asian Americans, Says Expert." *The Hill*. https://thehill.com/changing-america/respect/diversity-inclusion/489464-trumps-use-of-the-term-chinese-virus-for.

Soss, Joe, Richard C. Fording, and Sanford F. Schram. 2011. *Disciplining the Poor: Neoliberal Paternalism and the Persistent Power of Race*. Chicago: University of Chicago Press.

Stanfield, Kellin Chandler. 2011. "Persistent Racial Disparity, Wealth and the Economic Surplus as the Fund for Reparations in the United States." *Journal of Economic Issues* 45(2): 343–352.

Stanford, Shameka, and Bahiyyah Muhammad. 2018. "The Confluence of Language and Learning Disorders and the School-to-Prison Pipeline among Minority Students of Color: A Critical Race Theory." *American University Journal of Gender, Social Policy and the Law* 26(2): 691–718.

Stevens, Julia. 2009. "Child Development Accounts: Innovative Plans Build Savings for Youth, Starting at Birth." *Bridges*, April 1. https://www.stlouisfed.org/publications/bridges/spring-2009/child-development-accounts-innovative-plans-build-savings-for-youth-starting-at-birth.

Stewart, Carole Lynn. 2008. "Civil Religion, Civil Society, and the Performative Life and Work of W. E. B. Du Bois." *Journal of Religion* 88(3): 307–330.

Stewart, Gary. 1998. "Black Codes and Broken Windows: The Legacy of Racial." *Yale Law Journal* 107(7): 2249–2280.

Sullivan, Harold. 1981. "The Intent Requirement in Desegregation Cases: The Inapplicability of *Washington v. Davis*." *Journal of Law and Education* 10(3): 325–333.

Sullivan, Laura, Tatjana Meschede, Lars Dietrich, and Thomas Shapiro. 2015. "Less Debt, More Equity: Lowering Student Debt While Closing the Black-White Wealth Gap." https://www.demos.org/sites/default/files/publications/Less%20Debt_More%20Equity.pdf.

Sweeny, Joanne. 2019. "Incitement in the Era of Trump and Charlottesville." *Capital University Law Review* 47(3): 585–637.

Synnot, Marcia 2010. *The Half-Opened Door: Discrimination in Admissions at Harvard, Yale, and Princeton, 1900–1970*. Westport, CT: Greenwood Press.

"A Tale of Two Epidemics." n.d. Retrieved from https://wp.nyu.edu/ataleoftwo epidemics/.

Thein, John. 2004. *A History of American Higher Education*. Baltimore, MD: Johns Hopkins University Press.

Thomas, Hannah, Alexis Mann, and Tatjana Meschede. 2018. "Race and Location: The Role Neighborhoods Play in Family Wealth and Well-Being." *American Journal of Economics and Sociology* 77: 1077–1111.

Thomas, Melvin, Richard Moye, Loren Henderson, and Hayward Derrick Horton. 2019. "Separate and Unequal: The Impact of Socioeconomic Status, Segregation, and the Great Recession on Racial Disparities in Housing Values." *Sociology of Race and Ethnicity* 4(2): 229–244.

Tonry, Michael. 2010. "The Social, Psychological, and Political Causes of Racial Disparities in the American Criminal Justice System." *Crime and Justice* 39: 273–312.

Toussaint, Etienne C. 2018. "The New Gospel of Wealth: On Social Impact Bonds and the Privatization of Public Good." *Houston Law Review* 56(1): 153–221.

Traub, Amy, Laura Sullivan, Tatjana Meschede, and Thomas Shapiro. 2017. "The Asset Value of Whiteness: Understanding the Racial Wealth Gap. *Demos*, February 6. https://www.demos.org/research/asset-value-whiteness-understanding-racial-wealth-gap.

Ture, Kwame, and Charles Hamilton. 1992. *Black Power: The Politics of Liberation in America*. New York: Vintage Books.

Twine, France Winddance, and Charles Gallagher. 2008. "The Future of Whiteness: A Map of a 'Third Wave.'" *Ethnic and Racial Studies* 31(1): 4–24.

Tynes, Tyler. 2017. "Colin Kaepernick, Michael Vick, and the Fallacy of Respectability Politics." *SB Nation*, July 19. https://www.sbnation.com/2017/7/19/15990134/colin-kaepernick-michael-vick-and-the-fallacy-of-respectability-politics.

Tyson, Christopher. 2016. "How Did We Get Here: A Brief History of Black Baton Rouge." www.metromorphosis.net.

Valdez, Zulema, and Tanya Golash-Boza. 2017. "Towards an Intersectionality of Race and Ethnicity." *Ethnicity and Racial Studies* 40(13): 2256–2261.

Vaught, Sabina E. 2011. *Racism, Public Schooling, and the Entrenchment of White Supremacy: A Critical Race Ethnography*. Albany: State University of New York Press.

Visser, Nick. 2017. "5 Disturbing Statements by the Cop Who Shot Philando Castile." *Black Voices*, June 21. https://www.huffpost.com/entry/philando-castile-officer-interview_n_5949bddde4b00cdb99cb2c1c.

Wacquant, Loïc. 2009. "The Body, the Ghetto and the Penal State." *Qualitative Sociology* 32(1): 101–129.

Wallace-Wells, Benjamin. 2018. "How Cory Booker's 'Baby Bond' Proposal Could Transform the Reparations Debate." *New Yorker*, December 6. https://www.newyorker.com/news/the-political-scene/how-cory-bookers-baby-bond-proposal-could-transform-the-reparations-debate.

Wallerstein, Peter, ed. 2008. *Higher Education and the Civil Rights Movement: White Supremacy, Black Southerners, and College Campuses*. Gainesville: University of Florida Press.

Warner, Lloyd W. 1936. "American Caste and Class." *American Journal of Sociology* 42: 234–237.

Washington, Booker T. 1895. "Atlanta Exposition Address." http://wwphs.sharp-school.com/UserFiles/Servers/Server_10640642/File/bugge/Chapter%2017/washingtonvsdubois.PDF.

Weiss, Jana. 2017. "Remember, Celebrate, and Forget? Martin Luther King Day and the Pitfalls of Civil Religion." *Journal of American Studies* 53(2): 428–448.

Weller, Dylan. 2013. "Godless Patriots: Towards a New American Civil Religion." *Polity* 45(3): 372–392.

Whillock, Rita. 1994. "Dream Believers: The Unifying Visions and Competing Values of Adherents to American Civil Religion." *Presidential Studies Quarterly* 24(2): 375–388.

White, Bianca. 2018. "The Invisible Victims of the School-to-Prison Pipeline: Understanding Black Girls, School Push-Out, and the Impact of the Every Student Succeeds Act." *William and Mary Journal of Women and the Law* 24(3): 641–663.

Wilderson, Frank. 2010. *Red, White, and Black*. Durham, NC: Duke University Press, 2010.

Wilderson, Frank. 2003a. "Gramsci's Black Marx: Whither the Slave in Civil Society?" *Social Identities* 9(2): 225–240.

Wilderson, Frank. 2003b. "The Prison Slave as Hegemony's (Silent) Scandal." *Social Justice* 3(2): 18–27.

Williams, Kristian. 2015. *Our Enemies in Blue: Police and Power in America*. Oakland, CA: AK Press.

Wilson, Erika. 2016. "The New School Segregation." *Cornell Law Review* 102(1): 139–210.

Wilson, William Julius. 1978. *The Declining Significance of Race*. Chicago: University of Chicago Press.

Wilson, William Julius. 1987. *The Truly Disadvantaged*. Chicago: University of Chicago Press.

Wilson, William Julius. 1991. "Studying Inner-City Social Dislocations: The Challenge of Public Agenda Research: 1990 Presidential Address." *American Sociological Review* 56: 1–14.

Wilson, William Julius. 2010. "Why Both Culture and Structure Matter in a Holistic Analysis of Inner-City Poverty." *Annals of the Academy of Political and Social Science* 629: 200–219.

Winfield, Ann G. 2007. *Eugenics and Education in America: Institutionalized Racism and the Implications of History, Ideology, and Memory*. New York: Peter Lang.

Winters, Lauren. 2007. "Colorblind Context: Redefining Race-Conscious Policies in Primary and Secondary Education." *Oregon Law Review* 86(3): 679–731.

"World Conference against Racism, Racial Discrimination, Xenophobia and Related Intolerance." 2001. https://www.un.org/WCAR/durban.pdf.

World Health Organization. 2020. "Coronavirus Disease 2019 (COVID-19): Situation Report." https://www.who.int/docs/default-source/coronaviruse/situation-reports/20200413-sitrep-84-covid-19.pdf?sfvrsn=44f511ab_2.

"Wrestling with Respectability in the Age of #BlackLivesMatter: A Dialogue." 2015. *For Harriet*, October 13. http://www.forharriet.com/2015/10/wrestling-with-respectability-in-age-of.html#axzz52BO7pz5W.

Wright, Bruce. [1987] 1993. *Black Robes White Justice*. Jersey City, NJ: Lyle Stuart.

Wright, Earl, II. 2002. "Using the Master's Tools: Atlanta University and American Sociology, 1896–1924." *Sociological Spectrum* 22: 15–39.

Wright, Earl, II, and Thomas C. Calhoun. 2016. "Jim Crow Sociology: Toward an Understanding of the Origin and Principles of Black Sociology via the Atlanta Sociological Laboratory." *Sociological Focus* 39: 1–18.

Wun, Connie. 2014. "The Anti-Black Order of No Child Left Behind: Using Lacanian Psychoanalysis and Critical Race Theory to Examine NCLB." *Educational Philosophy and Theory* 46(5): 462–474.

Wyse, Jennifer Padilla. 2015. "Black Sociology: The Sociology of Knowledge, Racialized Power Relations of Knowledge and Humanistic Liberation." In *The Ashgate Research Companion to Black Sociology*, edited by E. Wright II and E. Wallace, 15–32. Burlington, VT: Ashgate.

Yalof Garfield, Leslie. 2014. "The Paradox of Race-Conscious Labels." *Brooklyn Law Review* 79(4): 1523–1567.

Yancy, George. 2018. *Backlash: What Happens When We Can Talk Honestly about Racism in America*. Lanham, MD: Rowman & Littlefield.

Yancy, George. 2000. "Feminism and the Subtext of Whiteness." *Western Journal of Black Studies* 24(3): 156–166.

Yearby, Ruqaiijay. 2018. "Racial Disparities in Health Status and Access to Healthcare: The Continuation of Inequality in the United States Due to Structural Racism." *American Journal of Economics and Sociology* 77: 1114–1152.

Young, Alford A. 1999. "The (Non)Accumulation of Capital: Explicating the Relationship of Structure and Agency in the Lives of Poor Black Men." *Sociological Theory* 17: 201–227.

Young, Alford. 2004. *The Minds of Marginalized Black Men*. Princeton, NJ: Princeton University Press.

Younge, Gary. 2019. "A 'No 10 Source' Is the Voice of Power. Too Many Journalists Simply Parrot It." *Guardian*, October 25. https://www.theguardian.com/commentisfree/2019/oct/25/deference-powerful-media.

Zewde, Naomi. 2018. "Universal Baby Bonds Reduce Black-White Wealth Inequality, Progressively Raise Net Worth of Young Adults." Working paper. https://static1.squarespace.com/static/5743308460b5e922a25a6dc7/t/5c4339f67ba7fc4a9add58f9/1547909624486/Zewde-Baby-Bonds-WP-10-30-18.pdf.

Zug, James. 2010. "The Italicized Life of Frank Wilderson '78." *Dartmouth Alumni Magazine*, September–October.

Zunz, Oliver. 2000. *The Changing Face of Inequality: Urbanization, Industrial Development, and Immigrants in Detroit, 1880–1920*. Chicago: University of Chicago Press.

Index

www.ingramcontent.com/pod-product-compliance
Lightning Source LLC
Chambersburg PA
CBHW020354270326
41926CB00007B/428